Kids on Skis

Also by I. William Berry

WHERE TO SKI

THE SKIER'S ALMANAC

KIDS ON

SKIS

Revised Edition

A Guide to Family Skiing and
Children's Equipment, Instruction, and Clothing

I. William Berry

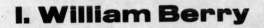

CHARLES SCRIBNER'S SONS
NEW YORK

To Dee, Greg, and Alix,
who made the book
not only possible
but necessary

Copyright © 1980, 1982 I. William Berry

Library of Congress Cataloging in Publication Data

Berry, I. William.
  Kids on skis, a guide to family skiing and
children's equipment, instruction and clothing.
  Includes index.
  1. Skiing for children. I. Title.
GV854.32.B47   1982   796.93   82–10460
ISBN 0–684–17782–X

1 3 5 7 9 11 13 15 17 19 F/P 20 18 16 14 12 10 8 6 4 2

Printed in the United States of America.

ACKNOWLEDGMENTS FOR THE FIRST EDITION

I couldn't have written this book without heavy cooperation from ski-area managers and ski-school/children's-program directors, and I thank all of the area personnel who've extended help and welcome for two full seasons and portions of three others. Since I was researching this topic simultaneously for this book and for a series of articles for *SKI* magazine—not to mention helping to formulate the new SKIwee program I discuss in Part IV—I'd like to offer special thanks to the magazine.

Since I needed depth as well as breadth, I ultimately had to focus on a few ski-area programs, and the two I selected for primary research were at Mount Snow, Vermont, and Copper Mountain, Colorado, areas with which I've long had a warm personal and professional relationship (translation: I like the people and the trails) and at which SKIwee was born. I've also spent considerable amounts of time at Waterville Valley, Loon, and Pat's Peak, New Hampshire; Sugarbush, Bromley, and Stratton, Vermont; Butternut Basin and Jiminy Peak, Massachusetts; Hunter Mountain, New York; and Keystone, Winter Park, and Vail, Colorado. While I don't agree with all facets of anyone's program, all these areas do an excellent job.

In addition, I've had help "above and beyond" the call of professional duty from several authorities on the subject of teaching children how to ski, all of whom helped even further by reading and correcting the initial draft of this book: Bob Kunkle, creator of junior programs at Copper Mountain; Tom Montemagni, director of junior programs at Mount Snow; Dr.

Don Overend, pediatrician and ski patrolman; Pam Stenmark, now associated with the Vail Seminar Center and previous director of the Copper Mountain Institute; and Norm and Gail Sweeney of Norm's Ski Shop in Keene, New Hampshire, especially for their help in Part II, Clothing and Equipment.

Over the years I've also received valuable tips, advice, and arguments from several other authorities: John Burrows and Rick Owen at Loon; Gary Andrus and Rick Godin at Copper Mountain; Judy Reiss and Martin Marnett at Sugarbush; Nancy Alfaro, Chris Diamond, Bruce McCloy, and Dr. Milton Wolf at Mount Snow; Werner Zwahlen and Ruth Chapman at Waterville Valley; Dave Chapman, Dave Currier, and Elliot Snow at Pat's Peak; Chan Murdock at Butternut; Brian Fairbank at Jiminy Peak; Kit Cooper (Chamberlain) at Bromley; Jeff Dickson at Stratton; Paul Pepe and the whole gang at Hunter; Dave and Barbara Roylance of the Winter Park Ski School; innumerable representatives of equipment companies, including the always helpful Carol Cone of Salomon; and Dick Needham, editor of *SKI*, without whose early support and conviction that this topic needed a thorough airing this whole project might never have emerged.

Finally, how could anyone do a book about "family skiing" without a family? My two children, Gregory and Alexandra, have borne up under the terrible pressure of being compelled to ski frequently with admirable élan, and my wife, Dee, is the one who keeps everything, including me, on target.

Lest anyone think this is all a subtle copout, all views expressed here are those of the management—meaning me. I may have tapped "the best minds of our generation," but in the final analysis, I made the final analysis and take all responsibility for it. On reflection, that isn't bad advice for a generation of young skiers to carry up the lift and down the trails along with their poles, goggles, and a delightful go-for-it attitude.

ACKNOWLEDGMENTS FOR THE REVISED EDITION

For a multitude of reasons, research on a topic like "kids on skis" remains ongoing, despite the fact that the first edition was just published in 1980. For one thing, I continue to monitor and write about SKIwee (and related topics, including junior racing) for *SKI* magazine; for a second, as equipment editor for *Skier's Advocate* I keep current on all aspects of that facet of the industry and, in fact, wrote a major article on kids' hardware during the 1981–82 season; for a third, I have these two "kids on skis."

As with any type of continuing research, most of the sources remain the same, but several new ones emerge and a few old ones depart. Okemo Mountain has replaced Bromley in Vermont on our regular itinerary, largely because it's a bigger and better mountain with excellent junior programs (and because we no longer need Bromley's first-rate nursery). We've received a lot of cooperation at Okemo from Ed Rock, Mike Potts, and Jim Remy, who do a fine job with youngsters at all levels of ability. We've added Pico, Vermont, just because we like it and because it has spent as much time dealing with young, serious skiers as has any place. It also has Frank Heald, one of the nicest and most competent area managers in the business, and who has a little experience of his own as a skiing parent and has some sympathy with my efforts to bring order out of chaos. What we've added at Mount Snow, Vermont, is a slew of brand-new "kids on skis" belonging to Chris Diamond and Bruce McCloy, which will keep them committed.

On the equipment front, I can't thank Bob Mignone of the Head-Raichle-Tyrolia combine enough. A skiing parent and director of a children's ski school in the Northwest before he headed east to work for RMUSA/AMF, Bob is not only willing but highly competent to discuss the problems of designing good equipment for youngsters. He and Tom Montemagni of Mount Snow are in the early stages of designing some testing methods, and I suspect that Bob's role within RMUSA has been at least partly responsible for the company's commitment to improving the breed. I've also received solid cooperation from Rick Howell of Geze (now allied with Elan); Keith d'Entremont of Fischer-Dynafit; Jean-François Lanvers, until recently the marketing director at Look; and Dave Scott of Blizzard. Overall, I sense some movement within the equipment sector as a whole to produce quality junior hardware, even though those items are rarely the high-profit models in a lineup.

Skiing being something of a high turnover business, some very good people with dedication to the junior skier have come and gone since the last edition, while others have changed jobs. Dan O'Connor and Bob Foster, two of the more perceptive marketing directors, have recently left Stratton, Vermont, and Waterville Valley, New Hampshire, respectively; I hope their replacements are as good. Gary Andrus has left not only Copper Mountain, Colorado, but also the world of skiing in favor of growing and bottling wine in Napa, California, which may prove a net loss to both industries, but certainly to skiing. Bob Kunkel also left Copper, but after a short sojourn in the real world of the telephone company (that's reality?) he came back, all forgiven, as marketing director at Winter Park, Colorado; however, Jerry Muth and Floyd Bashant keep Copper's junior program running at peak efficiency. Pam Stenmark is now director of publicity at Beaver Creek, Colorado, but remains committed to all levels of instruction.

For Butternut, Massachusetts, I would like not so much to add as to apologize for omitting ski-school director Einar Aas, president of PSIA, from the first edition of *Kids on Skis*. He understands as well as anyone how vital the teaching of youngsters is to the future of skiing and has been as helpful and cooperative as anyone I've worked with on this venture, as have Bob Schaeffer and Chan Weller at Sugarbush, Vermont, and the whole lineup at Keystone, Colorado.

Finally, I have to thank all of my fellow writers who plugged the first edition—is there a better way to say that?—in their columns, and those friends who have "lent" me their children from time to time for various program-testing purposes.

But, as always, the final analyses are mine, and I take full responsibility for them.

Contents

Introduction to the Revised Edition

Midway through March 1982, on a warm and beautiful spring day at Butternut Basin, Greg Berry, age eleven, blew his father off the hill. All season long, beginning with a two-day stint at the Mount Snow junior racing camp over Christmas, Greg had been narrowing the gap no matter how hard the "old man" tried to hold on, but that day, battling heavy snow, the kid moved ahead and took the crown.

His father, of course, is me, and I'd be lying if I didn't admit to having mixed feelings about the event. Or, for that matter, if I claimed I was conceding gracefully. Shortly afterward, I spent a few days at adult racing camps in Colorado, working under the coaching of no less than Billy Kidd and Otto Tschudi, and, for a short time after I returned, I pulled back even . . . maybe even a tad ahead. But on the last run of the season, mired in the heavier snows of May at Sugarbush North, I watched Greg absorbing what I had learned and, inexorably, blowing past me again. He is nothing if not a quick study, on the slopes as well as in school, and for all the innate competition between father and son I'm anxious to pass on all I know.

Well, almost.

Still, the distance between us isn't infinite and there will be days, in the upcoming season, when I will again nudge ahead: the right slopes, the right conditions, the right mood. But those days will become fewer and further apart. Greg has a naturalness with skis that I can never equal, because he started sliding at the age of two while I debuted at thirty-one, and as much as I hate to see the inevitability I had long accepted rationally (see the Introduction to Part I: The Beginning Skier, on page 3) actually occur, I'm now pleased I followed my instincts lo those many years ago and started him skiing almost as soon as he could walk. No matter what the experts told me then about starting a youngster too young (see Chapter 1).

By the time Alix, three and a half years Greg's junior, reached one and a half, the "experts" were beginning to waver a bit and concede—well, as long as you don't think they're *skiing,* it's okay to let them slide a bit on baby skis, but it is still wrong to take them down between your knees (see Chapter 7). It makes them too dependent, and they will never learn how to ski by themselves. Sure. Last season, on a beautiful February day at Pat's Peak, New Hampshire, Alix, then seven and a half, won her first Nastar bronze and would have hit a silver on her second run had she not hooked a tip on a gate right near the finish line. Dependent on me? When I asked what she'd been thinking about as she moved down the course, what invaluable tip of mine she'd been relying on, her answer was, "Viki Fleckenstein. I was thinking about how she would do it on that course, and then I did it as much like her as I could." Viki, the personable and successful pro racer who Alix had met a year earlier at Hunter and Stratton and again at Hunter a few scant weeks before her Nastar at Pat's, had replaced Dad as Alix's role model in the gates.

And so much for what the "experts" had said about that, too.

These days, in fact, my wife Dee and I are waiting for Alix to blow by us, which we're sure she will do at even a younger age than did Greg. Because, in the natural order of things, she isn't concerned about catching us; she wants Greg's derrière. Half his weight, on skis 40cm shorter, and physically nowhere near as strong, she hangs in his tracks for dear life and dreams of taking him. That's not going to happen so quickly, to tell the truth, but in the process of trying she'll leave Dee and me in the dust within another year or two.

And then, finally, Dee and I will be able to go off and ski alone—as we used to, before the kids arrived.

It's hard to believe that it all happened so quickly. A dozen or so years ago Dee and I were Every Couple, childless and carefree and just beginning to learn how to ski. Then the kids came and everything changed: We became Skiing Parents, and at times the hassles seemed to outweigh the pleasure; I often think we stayed with it those years mainly because I was in "the business." Schlepping infants around ski areas, looking for a decent nursery even in the early and mid-seventies was no bargain, and carrying them up the slope tucked under one arm so they could slide down could drive us up a tree. Many times, driving home from one of those days, we'd ask each other, "Is it all worth it?" Yes.

For one thing, both youngsters have grown up learning to live with mountains and snow and cold—to cope, as some would say, with an alien environment: They are, after all, basically big-city kids. For another, they learned to adapt easily to new places and people as I moved from area to area on assignments. For a third, Greg has learned, and Alix is learning, about caring for their equipment and clothing and handling money. In short, they've learned more about being self-reliant than they probably would have any other way.

They've also learned how to ski—slowly, naturally, easily, with no stress or pressure or feeling that they have to do it *now*. They started so young that they avoided the fear of failure or shame about falling; at that age falling was part of learning and playing. Now, when they fall, they regard it as a natural part of skiing. They stand up and laugh and brush themselves off and go back to sliding down the hill. Thus, I'm even more convinced today that what I wrote in the first edition of this book is true: The earlier you start children skiing the better off you—and they—are.

No matter what you think at the time.

Still, our generation, unlike that of our parents, has been called the "me" generation, with one basic credo: "What's in it for me,

Jack?" Sure, I can go on for hours about how much good all this is for the kids, which allegedly was our parents' primary concern, but I think it's also important to analyze what all this does for us.

To me, the biggest gain was the chance to know my children as other than a parent. Face it, how many experiences are there that a forty-seven-year-old man and an eleven-year-old boy and seven-year-old girl can really share? Skiing, of course, isn't the only one, but, like most of the others, it's an outdoor sport with both interior and exterior challenges, funny episodes you can laugh about together, and moments of fear you can discuss openly. Both Greg and Alix have been taught that it's perfectly all right to say, "I don't want to ski that trail" and that they'll find that apprehension respected; there are times *I* don't want to ski that trail either, and they've learned to respect that too (although Greg and Dee do, on occasion, square off on that).

Skiing with my kids has also widened my appreciation of skiing, by helping me learn to view a trail through another set of eyes: moguls that are molehills to me are mountains to Alix (and launching pads to Greg, who's been known to "get a little air" when he thinks I'm not watching). I've had to learn how to pick a line through a tricky piece of terrain that the kids can handle when they follow me, which is excellent discipline, as any competent instructor will tell you, and adds a bit of spice to a run.

Another gain, although this is more limited in appeal, is that it has radically changed my approach to the reportage of skiing. If nothing else, it prompted me to write *Kids on Skis* and to help expand the coverage of junior skiing in *SKI* magazine and *Skier's Advocate*—all of which was professionally helpful—and it increased my interest in junior racing (see Chapter 16), which I'd previously regarded as one big bore.

But it did more than that, because it forced me to look at skiing in a different light as well: what you learn by studying the junior "scene" has a tendency to overlap into the adult situations. Resort facilities, instructional theories, equipment and clothing criteria—understanding the junior problems has to increase your perceptions on a broader level. Just to give you a couple of examples:

* *Instruction.* When *SKI* editor Dick Needham and I both found out that we were fed up with how our children were being taught to ski, we created the machinery that ultimately led to the development of SKIwee (see Part IV for details). Our first approach, counseled by the handful of first-rate children's instructors we rounded up, was to exploit the concept of a "games" approach rather than a rote approach. When this proved extremely successful, we began to push for a similar program to help adults learn. It works.

* *Equipment.* When Alix expressed a strong preference for the Fischer Target over the Rossignol Jaguar, and Greg pronounced himself far more comfortable on a battered, used pair of Rossi Strato 105s than on a new pair of Kneissl Red Stars, I wondered if there was any unity of design to explain it. There was—the Target and the Strato have wood cores, and the Jaguar and Red Star have foam cores. Interesting, but was this universal or merely a random, small, and invalid sample? I started to reexamine my adult-testing selections, especially those I'd run under extended use (the only valid method), and guess what? Of my four favorite adult lines, three models—Head SL, Fischer SuperComp, and Elan RC08—had wood cores, while the fourth, Dynastar MV5, had a reinforced foam core. Further, two skis I'd originally liked but which proved unpredictable under extended use—the Rossignol FP and the Kneissl Red Star—had foam cores and had to be tuned more and more often to maintain the same level of performance,

while the wood-core models remained more constant. What annoyed me was that at one point I had known that, but had allowed some manufacturers of foam cores to talk me out of it—until Greg and Alix put me back on track.

In addition, I've had a lot of help, especially from Greg, in testing adult equipment—although my role hasn't always been completely voluntary. One thing qualified equipment writers tend to get is samples of new products that their promoters hope to see plugged (you think skiing is any different from any other business?), and some of these items used to get stuffed into a top drawer and forgotten. But Greg is a great gadgeteer, as are all boys, and as soon as I return home from one of the trade shows he asks, "Whadja bring back?" These samples are, of course, augmented by frequent purchases from our favorite ski shops or by visits to the lost-and-found departments of our favorite ski areas, since Alix can lose things between turns and, until recently, Greg wasn't much better.

As a result, Greg, with an occasional assist from Alix, has firmly proclaimed the following (my comments in parentheses):

* *Alpina* is the best ski goggle, while Scott—especially with the Star Wars ski mask attached—fogs too easily. Translation: Our initial fondness for the Scott in the first edition has waned. (I tend to have a similar preference for the rigid double-lens Alpina under extreme fogging conditions, like snow and rain, but I lean toward the softer single-lens Uvex under normal gray-sky conditions.)

* *The breakaway handle* is better than the strap (amen) —and to show he has no brand identification, Greg likes the Scott handle the best of any.

* *Aris and Grandoe* make the best mittens and gloves—
and you'd better believe he's lost enough of them to
have tried every @ #$% brand, type, and model out.
(And what Greg hasn't lost, Alix has).

* *Pullover parkas* (we opted for the Roffe) are the warmest ever (for which comfort he was cheerfully willing
to accept the slight problem of pulling it over his
head). Corduroy parkas aren't warm no matter how
pretty they are, but it took Alix the better part of the
season to admit that fashion, like virtue, isn't an adequate reward.

* *Chaps* are "the greatest things ever." Chaps, for those
of you who haven't seen them yet, are a most interesting version of over-the-boot gaiters for use with jeans
for spring skiing. Unlike the thin and all too tearable
traditional gaiter, these are zippered for ease of use,
are highly durable, lined for warmth and, for those
who care, reversible for fashion options. (Alas, I can
neither confirm nor deny nor even comment about
these. Although this was one sample I definitely had
planned to test, Greg attached them before I got
through the door and never relinquished them all
through the fall and spring seasons.)

* *"Afrika Corps" hats* are better than traditional wool
hats. (Here I can agree, because I smartened up and
came back from Austria with two of them, a white one
with a chin strap for me and a red one without a chin
strap for Greg. Greg, of course, decided that a chin
strap was necessary, so the one day I decided not to
wear the white one, he annexed it—but at least he had
the grace to trade me the red one.) These hats, for
those of you who haven't seen them yet, look like the
caps we used to wear walking around in the snow
when we were kids. They have bills and earflaps, are

waterproof, and are lined with down or fiberfill. Really quite efficient.

* *The perforated baseball cap* can't be beat—for spring skiing, preferably one reading "SKI," "Sugarbush," or "Molson Ale" on the front. (I agree totally, of course.)

Now, the astute among you will have noticed that I just sneaked a fair amount of information about clothing and equipment into this "introduction," which isn't usually where this stuff goes; it normally runs in the bulk of the book, right? Wrong, when you're doing a revision, as compared with a new edition. Doing a revision is akin to writing a new lead section on a major news story in a newspaper or magazine, making only the minimum number of "fixes" in the body of the story and doing nothing to change the "folio," or the arabic numbers on the pages.

Fortunately, the preface runs in the roman-numeral section and doesn't affect the main pagination. Thus, the "Introduction to the Revised Edition" becomes the "nu lede," as we used to slug the revision in my old newspaper days; and since the book's cover promises all manner of new information, I might as well continue with hardware. However, hardware is the one section of the book (Chapters 9, 10, and 11) I rewrote heavily, so the following are just "quickies":

* *Bindings.* Progress with bindings has been the best among all categories of junior hardware in the two years since the first edition. Tyrolia and Salomon, especially, have shown an enduring commitment to producing safe(r) bindings at all levels of weight, age, and competence, and my personal preference for Tyrolia is simply that: I prefer a pincer to a single-pivot toe (see Chapter 10). The two new junior models each company will produce for 1982–83—Tyrolia 80 and 40, Salomon 137 and 127 Mini—are by far the best products youngsters have ever seen and now surpass the Geze Olymp Junior, I feel. I see no need to buy the

smaller (40 or 127 Mini) of the two pairs; by the time a child is old enough to need a true step-in binding, the "heavier" (80 or 137) of the two (figure a minimum weight for the child of roughly 35 pounds) will do quite well. But—a crucial point—*none* of those bindings is really hefty enough for an aggressive youngster who weighs more than eighty pounds. For him, move up to the better light-adult models, such as the Tyrolia 280D, the Salomon 637, or, for people who prefer a rotamat, the recently discontinued Look 77C (translation: you should be able to get them at a decent price) or the new 99HP.

* *Boots.* I wish I were as pleased with boot developments as with bindings, but I'm not—at least, not for the kids. The *junior* boots—full-blown or scaled-down racing models for hefty kids like Greg—have come a long way and are virtually the equal of the adult models they copy: the Raichle Spyder (now the Grand Prix), the Dynafit Junior Comp, and the Dachstein Olymp are three to examine before making any choice in this area. But, below that, I'm still uncomfortable: I think virtually all of the boots for youngsters, even of Alix's size, much less the really little kids, are still too stiff and unforgiving. Sadly, what I felt was the best of this group—the Garmont series—has faded from the U.S. market, as of now, while the company sorts through the Italian version of Chapter 11. Raichle, Heierling, Dachstein, and Dynafit make perfectly acceptable models, but still have a way to go.

* *Skis.* Continued evolutionary progress is being made here, but, as with the boots, the *junior* models are superior to the *children's* models. Pick a company that makes a good adult racing ski and you'll find a good junior-racing ski: Atomic, Blizzard, Dynastar, Elan, Fischer, Head, *et al.* Make sure you opt for a wood

core (Atomic, Elan, Fischer, Head) or a strongly reinforced foam core (Dynastar's Omega, Blizzard's im-
pregnated fiberglass). With the next level of skier
(again, Alix's) the choice becomes tricky: Fischer's
Target (wood core) is excellent, but, mostly, the non-
racing models are foam-injected (known as "squirt
skis" in the trade) and therefore perform well for a
while but tend to break down. Actually, I can't think
of a children's ski with a wood core that retails for
much less than one hundred dollars—I may have
missed one, of course—which maybe says it all.

Since the "revised edition" promises updates of the best (and
worst) places to ski with children, I came up with a terrific way
to compile a new list. I handed Greg and Alix each a piece of
paper and told them to list their "top ten" areas. The theory
behind this was basic: The best places to ski with kids are those
the kids like best, because then they give you the least amount
of grief.

Both listed the same four areas in their top fives: Hunter
Mountain, New York; Loon, New Hampshire; Mount Snow,
Vermont; and Pico (in alphabetical, not preferential order).
Greg cranked in Sugarbush, Vermont, while Alix, who can't
handle that overall difficulty of terrain yet, opted for Waterville
Valley, New Hampshire (which ranked high in Greg's second
five). Their second fives were more diverse and included Butter-
nut Basin and Jiminy Peak, Massachusetts; Okemo and Pat's
Peak, New Hampshire; Stratton, Vermont; and Windham,
New York. Since I can't find fault with most of their choices,
let me make a few important points:

* These are all located in the Northeast, because that's
  where the Berry family skis; I don't take them west
  with me. However, for any skier located east of the
  Mississippi (including the greater Chicago area), the
  Northeast is as valid a vacation choice as the Rockies.

The overall cost is less, the ambiance is superior, and the quality of the skiing is virtually comparable. With good snow, uniform across the country, I had most of my "excellent" days of skiing during 1981–82 in the Northeast.

* Overall, the quality of children's instruction, from nursery through junior racing, is superior in the Northeast to that of the Rockies. The only Rockies resorts offering equal quality, best against best, are Keystone and Copper Mountain, Colorado, although Winter Park, Steamboat, and Vail in Colorado, and Jackson Hole, Wyoming, and Snowbird, Utah, are highly professional. However, virtually all areas in the Northwest have extremely strong children's programs (occasionally excluding the nursery), especially in the Greater Seattle region; one of SKIwee's regional supervisors, John Mohan, comes from Ski Acres, Washington. My recent impressions about California are strictly secondhand and, therefore, I'll take a pass —although people tell me that Alpine Meadows, Dodge Ridge (SKIwee), Kirkwood, Northstar (SKIwee), and Squaw Valley are on a par with any programs anywhere.

* Even within Greg and Alix's recommendations, all areas aren't identical. Mount Snow, Okemo, Pico, Stratton, and Waterville Valley are strong in all facets of area operation (snowmaking, grooming, lift maintenance), diversity of terrain, and junior programs. (My minor reservations about Stratton's nursery are detailed in Chapter 13.) Loon and Hunter are among the very best in the nation in area operations and diversity of terrain, with good and improving junior programs; however, both are a tad weak at the nursery level. Sugarbush is strong in area operations, tends toward the difficult in terrain, and has one of the best nurseries

in the country (and adult ski schools in the world) but is, paradoxically, still a bit weak in lower-level junior programs. (Racing there is handled by the famous Green Mountain Valley School.) Overall, all eight, by any set of criteria, are major ski mountains and serious resorts. Also, Jiminy Peak, Massachusetts, and Windham are excellent midsized ski areas, both in major expansion phases, with good facilities, programs, and accommodations, while Butternut and Pat's Peak are two of the best small areas in the nation by any set of criteria, with excellent mountain operations, reasonable diversity of skiing, and first-rate junior programs (Pat's racing setup is better than that of most major areas and Butternut's SKIwee program is exemplary).

* No, I haven't overlooked Killington or Bromley in Vermont, two of the region's most famous areas. Killington, in fact, may well be the most professionally managed operation in the country, on many standards, but it is owned by the same Sherburne Corporation that owns Mount Snow, which is head and shoulders better at the junior level (one of the nation's best, under Tom Montemagni) and which is the more family oriented of the two. Similarly, Bromley is owned by Stratton, which just offers a higher-level ski experience; although Bromley's junior program and nursery are at least as good as Stratton's, the level of terrain and the support facilities aren't.

* Other major northeastern resorts with respectable or better junior programs and adult ski experiences are Sugarloaf, Maine; Wildcat, New Hampshire; and Jay Peak and Burke Mountain, Vermont.

Throughout this introduction, I've touched and bounced off racing, so now let's bring it into sharp focus.

Junior racing has returned with a vengeance after a long

decline through the 1970s. Whether it's a result of the successes by the Mahres and Women's Team, as some feel, or just the fact that we now have a generation of kids who, like Greg and Alix, have been skiing since they were infants, as I suspect, is really irrelevant. It is a *fact:* Junior racing has not only returned but, more important, is again a significant factor in the development of junior skiers.

It has an even more important role than I discussed in the first edition of this book, which maybe says it all: The resurgence even in the past two years is verging on the "explosion" level.

Vermont is the king of junior racing and is important in several respects. No skiing state has more serious junior programs at more areas: Mount Snow, Stratton, Bromley, Okemo, Killington, Pico, Sugarbush (Green Mountain), Stowe, and Burke (moving from south to north) all field strong teams. Several also have high-school-age racing academies for full-time students. This doesn't mean that individual programs elsewhere in the nation aren't as good—Waterville Valley and Pat's Peak, Park City, Summit County, Squaw Valley, Sun Valley, a few in the Northwest—but rather that the Vermont Alpine Racing Association (VARA) is so strong throughout the state that the level of competition to which a youngster is exposed is uniformly high, tough, demanding, and serious.

Which, of course, is both good and bad.

Despite the growth in two years, my essential views about racing haven't changed since I wrote the first edition: For most youngsters, race training and low-keyed competition are good, while intense competition, amplified by a Little League syndrome, is bad. A few youngsters, of course, will thrive on that intensity, and from that cadre will come the next generation of U.S. Ski Team members. But that approach will ruin not only racing but also skiing for far too many other kids. To me, the purpose of bringing youngsters into the ski sport is to develop a lifelong recreational pursuit for them, not vicarious ego gratification for parents or cannon fodder for the Ski Team, and the purpose of race training is simply to make youngsters better skiers.

The ideal solution would be to develop race-training programs that control the intensity of competition. They call that utopia. Inevitably, what happens is that after the first flush of virtue, everyone—parents, coaches, resort personnel who finance all or part of the program—start asking, "Well, how good is that training *really?* How do we know it's so excellent?" Answer: "Look at how well our kids are doing against their kids." End of utopia.

We're all guilty of creating the system; me too. During Christmas week 1981–82, when I put Greg into a few days of race training because I thought he needed instruction in edge control and hand position, did I pick Mount Nowhere? Hell no. I put him into the program at Mount Snow because I know they have excellent coaching. How do I know (aside from, of course, insider knowledge)? Because in a few short years, starting from nowhere, Snow has become a major power within VARA and is producing a few winners. I also happen to know that Tom Montemagni, Wes Haight, and their coaches work very hard to maintain a balance between winning and instruction. But I also know that there, as everywhere, the pressure from the parents —who control the Ski Club/Ski Education Foundation (but fortunately, at Snow, not the coaching staff)—is to win, not teach.

Further, let's face it, ski areas rarely support a racing team or program purely out of charity. Ski areas compete with each other for business as hard as ski teams compete for victories, and the two forms of competition tend to be related. If Mount Snow is battling Stratton *(inter alia)* for adult business, the Mount Snow ski team has to do fairly well against the Stratton ski team because these days a big chunk of that adult business is family business and the hard core of skiing families have kids who race. These are the families that buy bonds or season passes and condominiums and are the families that become very important to early season cash flow (and to business generally, in a marginal-snow season). If these families are happy with the ski team, they tend to come back again and again, because their kids stay with racing a while, because they have other kids coming up behind them, and because they meet other skiing families with whom they have a community of interest. If they aren't happy, they go somewhere else.

Fortunately, new forces are emerging even within the serious-competition sector that may control some of the excesses. Many of the successful junior-program directors and coaches are upset at the official U.S. Ski Team hierarchy—especially at the talent scouts who try to raid the area programs for Development Team candidates—and at the underlying Ski Team philosophy that the future USST members must be selected at a very early age. These junior coaches, focusing on the same problems I identified in the first edition, in Chapter 16 on racing, want to keep their racers longer, giving them a chance to mature physically and emotionally and, perhaps, to put racing into a rational perspective.

The leader of this movement is one of the long-time authorities on ski racing, Warren Witherell, who runs the famed Burke Mountain Academy (and, frankly, should run the U.S. Ski Team). As Witherell sees it, the real progress will be seen in a few years when NCAA (collegiate) racing begins to reemerge as a parallel path to making the Ski Team. "Let's face it," he told me early in 1981, "World Cup racing is as much a professional circuit as the National Football League. Putting a group of young teenagers into that level of competition is bad enough, but telling them to win immediately or expect to get thrown off the team is criminal."

For him and for many of the junior coaches, using college skiing the same way the NFL does would be preferable, especially since—unlike swimming or gymnastics—ski champions are usually in their early twenties. However, if a youngster proves himself capable of competing on the World Cup circuit in his late teens, his college career can be modified to allow him to take off a winter term or two. But either way, "at least he'll have his degree when he's finished competing," Witherell says.

Will this system actually evolve? It's hard to say. Many of the racing establishment doubt it, but they have a vested interest in doubting it, since an effective NCAA ski-racing program would cut into the total authority now enjoyed by the Ski Team, the Ski Educational Foundation, the U.S. Ski Association, and, the big daddy, the International Ski Federation (FIS). But what will inevitably make it happen, one way or another, no matter what either side says, is that the explosion of new young racers will produce far too much talent for the current U.S. Development Squad/Team to absorb and this talent—especially the late bloomers—will filter upward through the area programs and the academies into the colleges; and like the current situation in VARA, the increased talent will increase the overall level of competition until it approximates that of the Europa Cup. In time, the NCAA stars will battle the Ski Team stars in the various national championships (spring series), and as the NCAA people gain a larger and larger share of the top-ten finishes the parity will be established. Until then, the Witherell forces can only dream; when it happens, USST will have no choice but to recognize it.

In the interim let's try to keep junior ski racing under control. If not, one option is to do what I do: As soon as he's good enough, put your child into a good racing program over Christmas to learn the fundamentals of good expert-level skiing, then put him back on the mountain in a lower-level "demonstration" program for the rest of the year and confine his competition to a few runs through Nastar. I'm not really satisfied with that, but it's the best of several bad alternatives I've found so far.

Finally, let's take another look at SKIwee.

As Chapter 18 details, and as I mentioned earlier, a few of us on *SKI* magazine were so annoyed at the poor state of children's ski instruction back in the mid-1970s that we decided to build our own system. This was necessary, we felt, because our children—mine and those of *SKI* editor Dick Needham, among others—weren't getting the kind of consistent, competent, and pleasant teaching we felt they deserved. But unlike most parents, we were able to do something about it. Late in 1978 we launched our pilot program at Mount Snow and Copper Mountain, ramrodded by Tom Montemagni and Bob Kunkel. For the 1981 season we had thirteen areas, coast to coast, in the fold, which we expect to expand considerably for the 1982–83 season. In addition, SKIwee had a five-minute special on the "Today" show early in 1982, and will be featured on another network during the 1982–83 season; has been written about in several major national magazines; and has finally convinced the Professional Ski Instructors of America that they have to do something about kids' instruction, which, in the final analysis, is even more impressive than the other two.

Even apart from that, SKIwee has continued to grow within itself as we refine it by addressing problems as they appear, since no program emerges perfectly formed, like Venus on the halfshell. SKIwee hired a national coordinator, Christi Northrop, who had written a book based on her experiences as a skiing parent and who used her children as guinea pigs, just as Dick and I had in those formative years. All of our children have now "graduated" past the SKIwee level, but we all continue to import new "subjects." In March 1982, for instance, I plunked one of Greg's closest friends, a youngster who'd never skied before, into SKIwee at Butternut, and by the end of the day he was an addict. (He was also alive and healthy, which was my original concern once I heard how Greg and Alix were planning to "teach" him how to ski.)

SKIwee's process is quite interesting, for those of you who have some feel for education. Obviously, the biggest problem any such program has is consistency of approach, especially as more areas are added: What, after all, does Jackson Hole have in common with Butternut Basin as a ski area? So, SKIwee decided to hold clinics at each area each season, run by Tom,

Bob, or John Mohan. The four of them—Christi, Tom, Bob, and John—confer each spring and summer on revision and content, then one of them runs the fall clinic at each area. During the season, Christi checks how well each area is performing and makes suggestions for improvement.

How well does it work? For all areas, the first season is the hardest. They join the program because they figure they'll get some free publicity from *SKI*—"We already have a good kids' program"—but halfway through the year, they begin to pay a bit more attention and, equally important, to modify several approaches and facilities. They appoint a director who, inevitably, takes it more and more to heart and begins to promote it internally for year two. By the third year it becomes an integral part of *area* operations, and by year four no one can believe they ever lived without it. By then, volume has swelled to where it really shows a profit, which convinces area operating and marketing folks to get behind it and commit to building that all-important terrain garden they should have had in year one.

You didn't really think it worked any other way, did you?

SKIwee also learned that report cards (details in Chapter 18) haven't worked quite as we'd expected—to allow immediate interchangeability between and among SKIwee areas—because, being kids, they lost or forgot the cards. (However, the kids *know* how well they did.) But it did have an unexpected dividend: It forced instructors to think about what, and how well, they taught, and it prompted many to tell us the card didn't go high enough into skills progression, which pointed to one inherent weakness (in the manual as well as the card) that was quickly solved.

Still, all is not perfection. We still haven't done as much with equipment as we'd hoped to, although we effectively discourage the use of unsafe and outmoded hardware, and we're still trying to figure out how to do some biomechanical research to find out what children's equipment should really be, as compared with smaller (albeit significantly better than it used to be) versions of adult models.

If all goes well, I should have something to report on these topics for the next revision. In the interim, we all continue to learn more and more about kids on skis. We've come a long way from the dark ages of just a decade ago, but we still have a long way to go. Fortunately, kids manage to survive even our mistakes, and the generation of youngsters we're now raising will, as Dick Needham often remarks, "blow our socks off." Unlike the first real generation of American skiers, those of us who came to the mountains in the 1950s and 1960s often as young (?) adults, our children have been on skis since they were infants and ski as naturally as they walk.

This, though, will provide its own challenges, because at eleven Greg is already as good as I am, and at twelve he will be better, and at fifteen—what? Will he and all the others like him need racing, freestyle, helicopters, and skiing out of bounds to intensify the experience and keep them interested? Will they find the controls we've created too restrictive? Will they seek new ways of testing their outer limits?

Probably. That's the history of generations as long as we've recorded it.

I've already seen enough signs of it, to tell the truth. Over Washington's Birthday vacation, the Berrys were skiing with Rick Owen, marketing director at Loon, former ski-school director at Wildcat, and one of the nicest guys in the business. "I know you've been telling Greg not to 'get air,' " Rick said to me, "but since he's going to jump the bumps anyway, shall I show him how to do it correctly?" "Go ahead," I said with parental resignation. Greg, who's always enjoyed skiing with Rick, quickly absorbed the idea of the correct line and anticipation, and, to tell the truth, by the end of the day even Dad was doing a little of that stuff too.

I mean, sometimes the little children shall lead, you know? Actually, *that* occurred on that last run of that last day of the season at Sugarbush at about one P.M., when the warm heavy snow of May had built into humongous moguls and ol' Dad was really fighting his way through. "The best line is over here on the right," Greg yelled, but this time I paid attention—unlike the episode a few years earlier—and, sure enough, he was correct. He also beat me down, but that's the way it is and that's the way it has to be.

Now, as for Alix . . . well, we'll talk about that in the next edition, as I wave her past me also.

Part I

The Beginning Skier

INTRODUCTION

I love skiing with kids—my kids, anyway. For one thing, Gregory—who was eight when I drafted this in the fall of 1979 and nine when I finished it—has forced me to continue to improve my skiing, no mean feat when you're in your mid-forties. For another, both he and my daughter Alexandra, now five and a half, have a directness that's refreshing after living for so many years in the adult world of euphemism. For instance . . .

Greg and I were skiing at Killington late in April 1979, and for some reason found ourselves coming down Great Eastern, which has an overall grade of descent of maybe 1 percent. The snow was heavy, the sun was warm, and the skiing was, to put it mildly, dull. Greg, of course, was skiing it properly: straight ahead, no turns, an occasional small wedge to reduce the speed to cruise-missile velocity. But I, the purported adult advanced skier, had to get fancy and short-swing through the slop—with the inevitable result: I caught an edge, fell, slid off the trail, and bombed into a tree about five feet below the lip—sharp pain in shin, skis hopelessly mired in deep slush, totally disgusted, but convinced (?) that no fracture had occurred.

"You okay, Dad?"

"Sure," I said, not nearly as certain as I sounded.

"Why don't you take off your skis?"

Just what I needed, helpful advice from my kid, especially since I'd been struggling to extricate the skis from the slop without thinking of his most obvious and perceptive solution.

But being, after all, a parent, I removed only one, tossed it back up to the trail (fortunately, I use ski brakes), then struggled to pull the other one up and out. I finally emerged, in pain but standing.

"You sure you're okay?"

"Yeah."

"Well," he said, looking up at me with a weighing look, "that sure was a dumb fall, Dad."

Amen. Still, as I skied the balance of the run back toward the lodge, I had to wonder how long he'd been storing that one up —getting even in one stroke for all of *my* "helpful" advice over the previous three seasons. Even worse, since it all occurred during the last run of the last day of the season, he entered the next season well ahead on points.

As did my daughter with my wife. Earlier that season, up at Waterville Valley, she'd suffered through another nursery/ski-school lesson of red-light/green-light, pronounced herself (at four and a half) totally bored with these lessons, and wanted to "go skiing." So my wife took her up on the J-bar to the top of the beginner slope, then listened with dismay bordering on tears as Alix told her, "Mother, I don't need you anymore." And sure enough, the little princess, with ponytail trailing behind her, negotiated the entire run herself. My wife Dee immediately made another adjustment, accepting the fact that soon she'd be fourth-best skier in the family, having been relegated to third the previous season one glorious day in March when Greg blew her off at Ascutney and became the top-ranked contender. (Dee has since decided to fight back herself.) One day, this season or next, Greg will take the title, but I continue to play King Canute as long as possible.

Competitive? This thing called family skiing? You bet it is. That's part of the fun. Skiing is one of the few life experiences in which you can allow a child to challenge you without losing authority if you lose the battle. In time, unless you happen to be a very young parent and a professional skier to boot, your children will soar past you, but if you handle it well you'll all benefit. Just as important, if you happen to be intelligent and aggressive, you can take advantage of the challenge to become a better skier yourself, delaying the inevitable just a bit longer. In doing so, you'll find yourself again skiing at your own outer limits, which, after all, is what skiing, and living, is all about. I refuse to accept middle age gracefully.

February 1980 offered a perfect example and proved that my crown is perched rather precariously. We'd just spent three days at Waterville Valley, with Greg and Alix testing the SKIwee program (see Part IV) while I checked the area's new NASTAR* clinic. Alas, I'd won a couple of medals during that workshop, and Greg was eyeing them more than somewhat . . . especially early the following day at Pat's Peak, when he noticed that a NASTAR was scheduled. "Can we, Dad, please?" he pleaded (since I had banned racing for him until he was twelve, for reasons I discuss in Chapter 16). I relented and signed us both into the race.

My first run was decent, good for a silver medal, but his first run was faster and, worst of all, good for the gold. "Oh, @#$%," I muttered to myself, because I'm nowhere near even close to good enough for a gold at my handicap; but could I let it pass? On my second run, I came blasting out of the starting gate, dropped into a tuck, came within inches of destruction at every gate as I skied about 80 percent faster than I ever had (or should), and all I could think was, "How soon, oh Lord? Do I hit the finish line before my thighs burn a hole in my ski pants, or do I catch a tip and break everything in my body?" Panting, hurting, and scared, I blew across the finish and heard, "Seventeen." "Gold?" I whispered. "Yup," came the laconic reply, and I turned to Greg and said, "We're retired until you're twelve."

"But Daddy," he said, "I still have one more run."

"But you already have a gold," I said.

"But you went faster," he said, "on your second run." And on his, he proceeded to come within one second of my best time. I don't like the odds for 1981.

* *SKI* Magazine's NAtional STAndard Race

This can be so much fun, so exciting, that it (pick one: always/sometimes/never-quite) overcomes the hassles of skiing with children. Because hassles there are. No matter how well or poorly they ski technically, children do silly things, they forget things, and mostly they do not have a stoic's discipline in the face of adversity, except at absolutely the wrong times— such as when they quietly get frostbite. Greg's adventures make me wonder if parents ever avoid the problems of skiing with children. No matter how long they've been skiing.

Dee read this and said, "Use that bit from Craig's column." (Craig Altschul happens to be my wife's favorite ski-writer.) Craig and his wife Peggi, who have no children, are sitting in a base lodge:

> One of [Peggi's] most exasperating "talents" is the ability to hear conversations at tables across base-lodge cafeterias. She always hears the ones that back up her contentions about the sport. She began to feed back the dialogue from a family four tables away from us.
>
> Mother: "If you two kids don't behave better, we'll never take you skiing again. Your socks are already soaked. John, do something."
>
> Father: "Whattaya want me to do? You're the one who wanted to take them. I didn't tell them to get their feet wet."
>
> The two kids were standing there bawling. Even I heard that without eavesdropping.
>
> To Peggi, that conversation was positive proof that people with kids should never ski.

As a parent, I can tell you that wet socks are a minor problem. If all problems could be solved as easily, skiing with youngsters wouldn't be a hassle. To solve this one, you simply jam extra pairs of socks (preferably two) into the kids' knapsacks, together with extra underwear, mittens, chapcream, hat, and goggles (plus, of course, the ski boots). *The* problem is to get the kids to carry the knapsacks, which by this time weigh as much as equipment to assault Mount Everest.

The *other* problem is that they forget where they leave their knapsacks—or mittens, goggles, dickeys, hats, parkas, skis, and poles (not to mention the combination to their SkiTote). At last count, Greg has had roughly thirty-seven pairs of goggles, although officially Alexandra owned thirty-six of them, because I precede each purchase with the statement to Greg, "I'm sick of buying you goggles you leave home, so I'm buying this pair for Alix but I'll let you use them today." Greg absorbs this with equanimity because he knows I won't let him go out without goggles, which is too bad because he hates wearing goggles over his eyes. He'll tolerate them around his forehead, holding his hat on, because they make him look like a skier; but use them for their designed purpose? He gets annoyed because I use glasses rather than goggles, so one summer I yielded and got him special ski-sunglasses to use for the season. He lost them by August.

My editor astutely asked, what about older beginning skiers, or even serious teenage skiers? They don't lose things, do they? Not having any firsthand experience, I called some friends who do. A few answers:

"She doesn't have any teenagers who ski, does she?" (No.)

"She's right. You don't worry about them losing mittens anymore. You worry about them losing skis."

"They still don't know enough to change wet socks, only you're not there to do it for them."

"@ #$%¢."

It's not just losing things. When Alix was four and a half she had this excellent pair of warm leather mittens, which did just fine until she went to one ski school that insisted she had to have poles. We gave her Greg's old poles, which was fine—except that she couldn't wrap those mittens around the poles. My first two solutions—"leave the poles home" and "learn to live with adversity"—didn't work. She got new mittens. If you know any child with small hands who'd like a good pair of barely used mittens, I know where you can get them cheap.

Equally annoying is that lack of stoicism, especially where what we shall delicately refer to as "calls of nature" are involved. Adults have learned a certain amount of discipline and/or planning, but with young children it's a "now" situation. Now, alas, usually occurs just as you're about to sit on the chairlift after a twenty-minute wait. Alternative situations, equally "now," focus on "I'm hungry," which can be offset by a melting candy bar in your parka, or "I'm cold," which is unbeatable.

In that same column, Craig also discusses Peggi's conviction that "couples shouldn't ski together." I'll pass on that—Dee happens to be a good skier—but if he had said "parents shouldn't ski together" he'd have had a point. This is especially true after you've dropped the youngest kids off in nursery or ski school. Just as you're about to get on the chair the mother says, "What time is it? How soon do you have to pick him up?" (We'll avoid discussing that "you" business.) If the father replies coolly, "How about tomorrow at four?" you've got grief. "Don't worry" is obviously the most inane comment you can make. All this is further compounded by the fact that mother has lost two or three seasons having the children and has yielded in skiing ability, which in turn . . . you get the point.

Despite all this, I have one firm, unwavering piece of advice on teaching children to ski: Start 'em early. The earlier the better. Get those dreary days behind you as quickly as possible.

Early? Yes. The age of two, or one and a half if that's the timeslot, is about right. (We'll discuss this in detail in Chapter 1.) You spend about $5 (it used to be less, naturally) for these little plastic skis, about a foot long with straplike "bindings," attach them to regular walk-around boots, and carry the kids maybe 100 feet up a gentle slope and aim them at the other parent, and believe it or not, they're skiing. If you're strong enough physically and technically, you take them up on a chairlift and let them ski down between your knees (I know a lot of the professional instructor types deplore this), and while your thighs burn from using an unaccustomed wedge you smile and say "whee" and "turn" and get them used to the movement and the rhythm and the sheer joy of sliding. Then one day, when they're maybe four and have graduated to the Yaller-Dragons and have suffered through nursery-school lessons, they toss their ponytail and say, "Mother, I don't need you anymore." And then they are really skiing.

Against this, many parents wait until their children are older, maybe ten or twelve or even eight, and in some ways this is too late. Not too late for them to learn how to ski well; given comparable athletic ability, if one youngster starts at two and another at eight, they'll be about even when they're ten. But think of all the fun you and they will have missed in those six years, not to mention the independence and confidence they would have gained.

Since I earn a fair portion of my livelihood writing about skiing, my kids have been bouncing among various eastern ski areas since they've been old enough to transport. Greg, who was born early in January, saw his first ski area that March, visited his first nursery the following November or December, played in the snow at Vail (his only western trip) when he was one, and was absolutely at home, completely comfortable, at any new ski area when he was three. By the age of five he was buying his own lunch and snacks, and he was skiing alone on selected (by me) short lifts and trails by the time he turned six. Alix started about a half year younger—and for a pair of city kids this confidence in an alien environment is something I wish my parents had provided for me. It's certainly added a solid dimension to my children's lives. Provided you control this exposure—and we'll discuss this later, also—you can create a sense of respect for and confidence in the outdoors.

In many ways, this is even more important than learning how to carve a series of perfect tight-parallel turns down Widow-maker—which youngsters are too smart to do anyway.

A large segment of this book—the final quarter—will focus on the skills and techniques youngsters are supposed to learn in order to master the challenge of downhill (or Alpine) skiing.

I'm of alternating minds—depending on the day, the weather, the phases of the moon, and how recently I've spoken to the head of a ski school—on how important it really is for a child to reach that "E" or "F" level of high technical proficiency. In my gut I feel that skills are essentially irrelevant to a young-ster's ability to *enjoy* what the public-relations folk call "the skiing experience." When a child's ready to master the next level of skills he'll do so, at his pace and adapted to his own talents and needs. But you must accept as gospel that when he's locked into a wide wedge, sitting back on the tails of his skis as he bumps down Jaws of Death, taking many spills along the way, he's *skiing*. And probably having at least as much fun as you are in your perfect comma position (if you're still married to that passé posture).

Why mention this? Because all too many parents feel their children should have the same hangups about form and tech-nique they do. Kids, frankly, think it's silly, if they think about it at all (which they usually don't, fortunately). Adults tend to pose, kids tend to ski. A few cases in point:

* A few years ago Greg and I were skiing with John Burrows and his son (two years younger than Greg) while John, a former racer, was marketing director at Loon (one of the best ski mountains in the country for youngsters to enjoy, by the way). Both kids were bop-ping down in what we'll call a wide-track wedge (al-though I've never seen quite that position illustrated in any teaching manual), totally abandoned to having fun. When I mentioned casually that their form left a tad to be desired, John simply yelled down the hill, "Stop." Both instinctively leaned knee and hip into the hill, lifted the nonturning ski, and stopped almost im-mediately. "See?" John said. "They have as much nat-ural edge control as you and I do, so why screw up their heads with nonsense?" Point made, point ac-cepted. To underscore a parallel point, John, who can

blow me off the hill the best day I ever saw, skis with his boards a lot farther apart than I do. And a lot stronger edge.

* Tom Montemagni, who heads the junior program at Mount Snow (one of the best in the country), tells of the day he had one of the area's best adult instructors work with a group of advanced young skiers. "The drill was to get the kids out of a stem earlier and earlier, so that they finally made a strictly parallel turn. So run by run he narrowed the stem and got his skis parallel earlier, and the kids dutifully copied exactly what he did. By the end of the lesson they were making beautiful parallel turns. Then the lesson ended and the instructor left—and the kids went right back to making stem turns and skiing the way they felt comfortable."

I could offer a few more examples, but perhaps the comment made by Bob Kunkel, who created the excellent kids' program at Copper Mountain, is about as incisive as any: "The biggest obstacle to kids' learning how to ski well is their parents' expectations." Or, as Montemagni said, "Kids just aren't as concerned with getting their money's worth out of every lesson." Whichever way you look at it, just don't get hung up on your kid's skiing in a tight parallel. The day I see Greg skiing with both skis consistently pointing the same way and/or near each other I'll keel over and faint—yet he can keep up with me on most blue-square trails, can ski as long a day, and has a lot more fun. For the most part, he skis under control. Even when he does sneak in a jump over a bump when he thinks I'm not looking.

None of this is meant to suggest that all is chaos in teaching youngsters how to ski—or, more accurately, helping them learn how to ski (a signal difference). The good junior programs—Mount Snow, Copper Mountain, Keystone, Vail, Waterville Valley, and many others—have a definite progression of skills that should be acquired somewhere along the way, focusing primarily on balance, edging, body position, and, ultimately, initiation. It doesn't focus much on wedges and stems and parallels, which are more a residue of the archaic, Austrian-inspired Modified American Technique with which I, and probably you, first learned how to ski. Today's theory is more concerned with independent leg action and weight transfer than with "unweighting" and "final forms." Its aim is to produce strong skiers with different weapons to be used in attacking different terrain problems—when, and only when, that skier is ready to learn the next skill, to master the next weapon.

The best new programs, in Montemagni's words, are "child oriented." They accept that different children have different capacities to learn, to advance, and to excel, and the instructors and directors try to adapt the programs to each child. "Al the Athlete and Tubby Tommy just cannot progress at the same rate," he says. "Why can't parents learn that?"

Partly, I guess, because we are parents, imperfect human beings in a less than perfect world. If my first piece of advice is "Start them early," my second is "Leave them alone to learn at their own rate." I just wish I could follow my own advice, because when Greg reads this he'll give me one of those funny looks kids reserve for what the Indians identified as "speaking with forked tongue." I mean, we all know *why,* that day on Great Eastern, he couldn't help but comment, "Gee, Dad, that was a dumb fall."

For all the technical focus included in this book—equipment, clothing, instruction, schools, and areas—many of the situations we meet in skiing with children involve plain common sense. If the demographics the industry passes around are accurate, skiers as a group are young, well-educated, affluent . . . all those good things. Yet somehow, all too many parents seem to leave common sense home with the bills when they head for the hills. Before we dig into the complexities, let me leave you with a few general rules:

* Clothe thy children as thyself (detailed in Part II). They have to stay warm and they have to be able to move, or else they can't ski. This applies to equipment as well: a six-year-old will do as well as an adult on ice with dull (or nonexistent) edges. Don't look for bargains.

* Put them in school, unless you happen to be a certified instructor—at which time you already know enough to put them in school without my saying so.

* Teach them the rules of the slopes: courtesy, safety, and respect for their environment. I shouldn't even have to mention this, but I see an awesome number of children who haven't been taught.

In the past few years, in fact, I've seen many children who terrorize the slopes and put both themselves and novice/low-intermediate adult skiers in danger. I've seen kids doing silly if not downright dangerous things on chairlifts. I've seen children run into lift-towers, and the 1978–79 season saw several young teenagers killed slamming into trees because they were skiing far too fast on expert slopes and lost control.

Face it, skiing can be a dangerous sport—which is, after all, part of its attraction. Mountains, snow, extremely cold weather are all alien elements in most of our urban/suburban white-collar worlds, which again is part of the lure of skiing. But the line where danger passes from exhilarating to suicidal is a tough one for adults to define—that classic "ten/tenths"—and impossible for children. Unless they're taught. As parents, that's our job. We can't pass it over to the ski school or the ski patrol. We have to teach our children to respect, but not fear, those alien elements and the other skiers. To me, that's a big part of the "ski experience."

Fortunately, the newer ski-school programs—such as SKIwee, which we'll discuss in Part IV—are addressing some of these problems. But that alone doesn't excuse or exculpate a parent who doesn't teach and reinforce these rules of safety.

This book swings a wide loop over the entire area of children's instruction, but inevitably a few aspects are shaded to reflect a few decisions, analyses, research pragmatics, and, inevitably, biases on the part of the writer. As I reread the entire manuscript after getting the original draft back from my panel of experts, I caught a few such items that should be discussed casually here.

BIG-AREA BIAS

As I suggest in Chapter 5, I prefer to ski on big mountains with 2,000-foot (give or take a few hundred feet) vertical drops. I also like ski areas with sophisticated support facilities for adults (a good restaurant as well as a cafeteria, a nice bar, a first-line ski and repair shop), as well as top-notch programs oriented toward children. This tends to permeate my total coverage of this topic. My main research was done at big areas, and inevitably my experts were based at those resorts.

Let me make one crucial statement here to offset this subliminal impression that big areas are better: Some of the smaller ski areas often do as good a job, possibly even a better job, in teaching children how to ski and in developing programs in racing, freestyle, and junior-instructing and -patroling to entertain the strong junior skier. I've been especially impressed by the programs at Pat's Peak, New Hampshire; Catamount, West, and Willard mountains, New York; Butternut Basin and Jiminy Peak, Massachusetts; and Bromley, Vermont (which is really a small mountain). In one way or another they all offered total cooperation, and the one area whose hospitality I accepted for in-depth research—Pat's Peak—convinced me that these small areas can do a big-time job with kids for far more reasonable fees. In addition, several have indicated a strong interest in joining SKIwee (see Part IV). Therefore, on balance, if your primary interest is to find a ski area with good programs for your children, don't automatically aim at a big mountain; if, however, you're a serious skier yourself, think twice about signing on for a protracted period with a small area.

SERIOUS-SKIER BIAS

As I suggest consistently throughout the book, my wife is every bit as serious—and almost as strong—a skier as I am. The only reason I'm a stronger skier is because I log a lot more mileage on assignments for *SKI* and other magazines, have been through several advanced-skier workshops, and didn't lose two seasons having children. She enjoys skiing even on marginal-conditions days, uses top-line equipment, and likes to point them down the hill and let them run. Thus, the book has this perception as a built-in bias.

Although this pattern is true to greater or lesser degree among some of our friends, it's totally absent among others, where quite often the husband is either by far the better or the only skier in the family. This latter tends to be unfortunate for the children, because—an interesting paradox—youngsters in families where neither parent skis are more apt to log a fair number of ski days than those in families where only one parent skis (or skis seriously). I'll discuss this total situation in Chapter 3, but I wanted to mention it now as well.

TWO-PARENT BIAS

My wife and I have been married for a number of years and intend to keep spittin'-snarlin'-and-battlin' our way through for another significant number of years. Virtually all of our close friends fall into the same pattern—the gathering of an endangered species, I'd suspect. Thus, we tend to view skiing as a two-parent, two-child venture and usually log at least twenty days a season in this mode (see Chapter 6), and there's no way this isn't going to permeate my approach to skiing.

At the same time, Greg and I have gone off together on an average of two or three days a season for several years now, and we find it quite enjoyable; and Alix and I had fun in March 1980 on our first "solo" trip. I know other ski-writers who do this far more frequently. Personally, I can think of few participant activities where a thirty-six-year age gap is less noticeable than winging down a trail together, and I expect this to survive until Greg discovers that skiing with girls is even more fun. Also, while I've been going out west every March for years on a story swing (my perennial alibi for cutting tracks in Rocky Mountain powder), Dee has taken both Greg and Alix skiing by herself with equal enjoyment. Thus, I can tell the single parents among you that I'd have no problem taking either or both children with me for a full skiweek—and if anything, I'd imagine it would be even easier to do on a learn-to-ski basis. It's certainly something I'd recommend without hesitation. I'll discuss this, too, in Chapter 3.

SKIING-IS-A-GOOD-THING BIAS

After more than a decade with *SKI* magazine and with three books about skiing under my skis, I think we can assume that bias. What I like about skiing isn't only the obvious—the thrills and spills—but also the fact that it's a lifelong pastime (I have friends in their seventies who still slide regularly and well) that gets you out of doors on cold, brilliant days, away from the TV set, to recharge the batteries so that you can face the workweek physically and emotionally fit. And for all the hassles of getting that family-of-four (more or less) onto the slopes, the lost goggles and the wet socks and the high price of hardware, skiing is still the best family venture we've found. And I don't care what the rest of my family says.

Photo courtesy of Vermont Ski Area News Bureau.

"Whenever the child is ready."
DR. DON OVEREND,
pediatrician and ski patrolman

"When his parents are ready to accept the responsibility."
TOM MONTEMAGNI,
junior program director, Mount Snow

"Kids learn to ski because no one tells them they can't. Kids learn to ski because they're good beginners. And why not? They're beginner people."
BOB KUNKEL,
creator of children's programs, Copper Mountain

1

HOW OLD
SHOULD THE CHILD BE?

Greg hadn't even been born when I started asking friends in various ski schools across the country, "When should he start skiing?" I'd like to think this curiosity and concern was mostly on Greg's behalf (or my wife's), but I often suspect the truth might have been otherwise. The last thing I wanted when I headed for the slopes (on assignment, of course) was grief from distaff quarters, especially since my usual comment—"You know I'm working when I'm skiing"—has never had much success within my nuclear family. The sooner I got everyone on the boards the better off I'd be.

Obviously, January 8, 1971 (the day Greg was born), was a bit early, but under current theory January 8, 1972, might have been fine. Tom Montemagni reports that one avid skier put his nine-month-old son on skis when he took his "first tentative steps." Certainly, January 8, 1973, was all right. Alix, our younger child, was on skis when she was one and a half, and by four and a half she had managed to negotiate the full length of Snowshed at Killington by herself. Although as recently as the early 1970s the theory was still "no one can ski until he's six," the theory has proven itself wrong. Since it still lingers in parental thinking like boilerplate under a fresh Vermont snowfall, let's say it right now, out front: There is nothing mystical about the age of six, or five or four or three or ten or fifteen. As far as beginning to ski is concerned, no minimum age exists. A child can start whenever he and his parents are ready.

Parental "readiness" is important. I once wrote an article

noting that the year Greg turned six, everything ski instructors and I had been trying without success to teach him the previous season just "clicked in" one weekend in December. It did happen that way, because that was the week I finally bought his first pair of real skis, with inset edges, and good bindings. In other words, *I* was finally ready for Greg to start skiing "for real," so of course he responded. I suspect he'd have done the same at five had I been ready, possibly even at four. We'll never know, of course—that's the problem with self-fulfilling prophesies.

Still, as Dr. Don Overend has commented, much depends on what you and your child mean by *skiing*. Gary Andrus, former marketing director of Copper Mountain, tells of the day his three-year-old daughter caught him on his way out to work and said, "I wanna go skiing." "So," he said, "I stopped everything, got out all the clothing, bundled her up, strapped on the little skis, took her outside, and said 'Go.' She went maybe the length of this room, turned around, and said, 'I'm done.' Maybe you and I might not think she went skiing, but she sure thought she did."

This is a very telling point. At ages two and one and a half respectively, Greg and Alix were skiing. By their lights. Sometimes my wife and I would strap on those hideous blue plastic foot-long *things* (I really hate to call them skis) and aim the kids from one of us to the other; other times I'd take them up in a chairlift (how they both loved that!) and ski them down a gentle slope between my knees (my thighs, my thighs), getting them used to the feel and motion of turning and running straight. After maybe a year of this a gradual change occurred: They became willing, on gentle terrain, to ski alongside me—holding on at first, then, in time, venturing solo. (This usually coincided with shifting to 90-mm Yellow Dragon solid-plastic skis.) Sometime during that season they'd take their first nursery-school ski lesson, learning not so much technique or skills as independence, just being able to walk around by themselves, then climbing, then sliding, then wedging.

From the first day those yucky plastic things were strapped to their regular walkaround boots, they were skiing. From then on, it was simply a matter of improvement, graduating to better equipment, and developing confidence, independence, and skills. There was, in short, nothing magic, nothing mystical, that season Greg turned six. As with all kids, his learning process hasn't been a smooth, inexorable upward line. A child's progression in anything is always erratic and random, and during that one weekend early in the season he suddenly learned, or rather put together, a whole mess of different things he'd been taught during the previous season. Since then, he's plateaued and jumped and plateaued again and jumped again, as I imagine he will continue to do. However, to pick any one jump, or plateau, and say, "That's when he started *skiing,*" misses the point. He started the first day he strapped on those yucky skis.

Still, not all children are ready to do even that at one and a half or two, or four or six or eight. Pushing them, all experts agree, is courting disaster. They'll do it if you really insist because it's *you* who's insisting, but they'll fight it all the way and, worst of all, they'll hate it. Better to put them in a nonskiing nursery, with toys and other kids to play with, and wait for the day *they ask* if they can go out to ski with you or take a lesson. That's the day they're ready to start skiing.

Pam Stenmark, who's been actively involved in children's teaching programs at both Copper Mountain and Vail, adds one cautionary comment: "Don't start at two unless you plan to take them skiing several times that season, or at least take them out for snow-play in the backyard. Kids that young need so much repetition and skills reinforcement that one or two days are essentially a waste of time—unless the parents treat the whole episode as just play, not a ski lesson."

A reluctance at any age to start skiing doesn't mean your child is backward, a coward, or any such foolishness. Judy Reiss, who heads the excellent Valley Day School at Sugarbush, Vermont, comments astutely, "Many city kids are just overawed by all that snow, those big strange mountains, the cold and the color and the funny clothing people are wearing. You can't expect a city kid like that to want to ski the first day he's there." In contrast, children raised in the mountains—or, like mine, who have virtually lived at ski areas since they were born —find nothing alien or frightening in that environment.

Stenmark draws another distinction, that between the physically active child, "one who's into games, movement, risk, and challenge at an early age," and the more passive youngster "who reads and watches TV or is generally quiet." The former, "those who are confident and outgoing, will do much better in early skiing situations than those who are shy and easily frightened." Parents who can spot these signs, she says, "will do themselves and their children a good service if they honestly accept the signs."

Perhaps this explains why even a few ski-area-bred children take their time venturing out. Many, like John Burrows's son Aaron (when John was marketing director at New Hampshire's Loon Mountain), can bomp right on down a black-diamond trail with a wicked wedge at four, but I know the daughter of a director of skiing elsewhere in the Northeast who eschewed skiing as late as six. "Closest she came *that* season," he told me later with a laugh, "was when your son [a year older] said to her, 'Let's go skiing.' That almost did it." Fortunately, he never pushed, and when she was finally ready, she went skiing. She'll do fine.

But some have pushed, and the son of one of America's top ski-school directors was an absolutely dynamite skier by the time he was seven or eight—and completely burned out at eleven.

So, as the good doctor said, a child is ready to ski when *he's* ready to ski. That is the mystical age. Let the child set the pace and define skiing for himself. As we'll discuss in detail later, keep your own definitions, timetables, and hangups to yourself.

However, there is a satellite question: How old should he be before he takes his first formal lesson? The answer's essentially the same, except that ski school is *school.* One reason the former five- or six-year-old rule for beginning existed was because that was the age at which most children started real school and, therefore, would be familiar with classes and teachers and interaction with other children. This still holds: A child shouldn't take a lesson, either from ski school or from the nursery, unless he's been in school. But these days, many of our children start regular nursery school (even play groups) when they're three or four, which means they're ready for a ski lesson. If they feel they are.

"So he wasn't from Kansas City. So he was from Omaha."
BOB KUNKEL

"Kids are so filled with sugar at ski resorts, with hot chocolate ten times a day, that they have a variety of reactions that all make it difficult for them to learn."
TOM MONTEMAGNI

"If your children can't tell you what they learned in words, have them draw pictures about it."
BARBARA ROYLANCE,
director of children's programs, Winter Park

2

WHAT CHILDREN'S PROBLEMS MUST YOU SOLVE?

On a glorious Monday in March 1979, Bob Kunkel and I were trailing a group of kids in Copper Mountain's ski school, just watching how the class did. We saw this one boy, maybe ten or eleven, continually staggering, falling, having trouble getting up, and, all in all, not keeping up with his class. "I bet you," Kunkel said, "that he and his parents drove straight through from Kansas City yesterday, didn't stop for sleep, had a doughnut and coffee for breakfast if that, and barely got here in time to sign up for school."

How could I fail to cover that bet? So we skied over and helped the kid to his feet, and Bob began to question him gently. Sure enough, the smart-guy writer from New York got hustled again; over margaritas (my treat) that night, Kunkel said, "I almost hate to take your money. It happens that way so often you wouldn't believe it. Parents just don't know how to handle a skiweek with kids."

Or, for that matter, a ski day or a weekend. If there's one place where this "kids are kids, not little adults" manifesto holds true without qualification, it's in the fact that children have a lower level of tolerance on a lot of levels:

* *Change of plans.* If you tell your youngsters you're skiing Pat's Peak on Tuesday, neither rain nor snow nor excess at night had better keep you from that appointed round, as my wife informs me regularly. I have a tendency, like many adults, to "hang loose"

and change my plans at a whim's notice. My "story run" may have me at Copper Tuesday and Breckenridge Wednesday, but I'm quite apt to waken on Wednesday morning and say, "I'm stayin' at Copper today because (fill in the blank, but it all reduces to, because I want to)." I may also waken and decide I don't feel like skiing that morning at all because I've put in four hard days in a row and the world won't come to an end if I read for a few hours and don't hit the slopes until noon. I'm sure you've done the same thing—but don't try it with kids. They are rarely flexible on schedule, promises, and anticipation.

* *Change of regimen.* Children need sleep, breakfast, lunch, dinner, snacks, and TV time as much on a skitrip as on a regular school day, as close to the same schedule as possible. Unless your children are used to driving late at night, that kind of saddle-up-for-skiing trip can be seriously disruptive. If they regularly eat on a 7-12-6 schedule, shifting by even an hour can be uncomfortable, which is one reason why ski-area cafeterias get so crowded at noon. Maybe you and I can skip lunch on a ski day (or juggle it to 11:30 or 1:30), but youngsters can't. They're also less tolerant of eating a "great dinner" at 8 P.M. (especially compared with hamburgers at 6 P.M. at McDonald's).

* *Change of diet.* This is one place we're all guilty, me as much as the next parent: We let our children get away with eating junk food and too much refined sugar, far more than we'd ever allow at home, because those hot chocolates and candy bars are the easiest "quick hit" with which to push them back out onto the slopes. "We've all overlooked this problem," Tom Montemagni said in January 1980. Tom is a serious marathon runner as well as a ski instructor and has

been following the changes in running diets quite closely. "Look at the deer," he said. "When the snow gets too deep for them to eat grass, they eat the bark off the trees. This fills their stomachs, but they lack nutrition, and if they suddenly have to run hard they can drop dead in their tracks. The same type of thing can happen to children because they're filled with sugar. This makes for difficult learning with reactions like hyperactivity, listlessness, fatigue, inability to concentrate, et cetera. So instead of that hot chocolate and candy bar, why not a milk break or a fruit break or a cup of hot soup?"

* *Nonstop skiing.* An experienced adult skier in decent shape can keep going all day, especially on those "perfect" days when sky and sun and snow and temperature are just right. I often stick a couple of candy bars (for *me;* I'm not Tom) in my parka pocket and nibble on the lift, rather than stop for lunch. Right? Well, don't try that with children. They do tend to ski nonstop and quickly, but when they tire, which occurs with amazing suddenness, it's time to quit. At that point, they cannot ski anymore until they've rested inside the base lodge, preferably over a hot chocolate (sorry, Tom) and a piece of fruit, after which they can go out and bomb nonstop for another hour. The pattern repeats inexorably.

* *Stopping while skiing.* Conversely, when they're skiing they want to *ski,* which does not include frequent stops along the trail to look at the pretty landscape. Exceptions do exist: If you find a tree with bear-claw marks twelve feet above snow level, you can't get children away from it. Aside from that, things like sudden changes in terrain, patches of ice, or a Normandy of fallen skiers will not deter kids from their appointed rounds with the chairlift.

* *Extreme weather and snow.* This should be rather obvious, but based on what I see and hear it isn't. Youngsters can and will get frostbitten on days you and I won't even regard as being cold. They also get overheated (and tired) more quickly on warm spring skiing days, and more worn out by heavy snow. (Conversely, ice bothers them less than it does most adults of comparable ability.) The problem is, some kids won't tell you they're cold, warm, or even getting tired when they're *on the trail,* as compared with on the liftline or at the base. They rarely sense they're getting frostbitten. This whole area of weather-conditions tolerance is one a parent (or instructor) has to watch very closely.

* *Concentration* or *attention span.* Good instructors and program directors have known about this forever, but parents often fail to notice that their child has lost his concentration. As with the weather, a parent has to learn how to look for the warning signs: a couple of silly-type falls (you recognize them in time), a regression in technique (ditto), meandering eyes, things like that. You can tell him from now until doomsday to "pay attention," but you're talking to yourself; his concentration is blown, period. It is far better to recommend stopping for a hot chocolate. (Habits die hard, Tom.)

* *Words, words, words.* Unlike adults, who thrive on analysis, children don't like being told how to ski. (We'll talk about this in detail in Part IV.) You don't explain to a child how to play, and skiing is play. And play, as a psychologist has commented, is a child's work. They respond to games, images, sounds, even a simple "follow me," but their eyes glaze when you go into technical explanations. So don't waste your breath. On a related problem, Barbara Roylance of

Winter Park has commented that children often have trouble using words to explain what they have learned. "But drawing pictures is another game," she says, "and children are often very accurate in showing you what they learned and how they should be standing on their skis. It's also a good way to reinforce what they learned."

* *"Fine tuning."* One thing again that instructors (and physicians) understand that parents often don't is that children cannot execute certain movements on skis because they aren't physically capable of it. Children develop big-muscle dexterity first, and often have tremendous (relative) strength in their thighs, for instance. But they often cannot make the subtle adjustments with their hands and feet that an adult can, and they have to adapt their technique/skill development to accommodate what they can and cannot do. As a parallel problem, their coordination isn't as good as that of adults, and often the reason their pole plants are so terrible compared with their other skiing skills is because they can't coordinate the sequence.

* *Unfamiliar places.* Children also, as we've suggested, have far less ability to adjust to a new environment. This not only refers to skiing as such but, equally important, to each new ski *area* itself, unless or until they've skied a lot of areas and don't regard each as a new experience—when, in short, they know where the bathroom, cafeteria, and meeting place will be. Until your child reaches that point, run through the familiarization drill at each new area just as you did the first time you all went skiing.

This brings up the question of whether you should ski with your children, let them ski alone, or deposit them in ski school for the day. Perhaps I'm the wrong person to answer it, because I find my youngsters' reactions and alibis (for whatever) fun, interesting, different, and challenging. I often let Greg or Alix pick the trail and lead the run; it gives them a sense of responsibility and acceptance (and me a chance to watch how they're skiing).

However, Greg does like to take a few runs by himself (so he can sneak in a few jumps or hook up with another kid for some ad hoc racing), and that's fine too—provided you set the parameters: I tell him which trails and lifts he can ski, and arm him with several firm rules, such as lowering the safety bar, not riding a lift alone, and not playing on lifts. I also give him a time by which he must be back at a central meeting place, unless I tell him I'll meet him at the bottom of the lift. I also make sure he carries identification, some money, and a few other things we'll discuss later in detail.

Why let them ski alone when it can be dangerous? It helps them to develop a sense of independence and responsibility as well as giving them a chance to go off and "do their own thing," learning "what works" without having you hanging over them. It has to be done carefully: You have to scout the lifts and trails and have a realistic appraisal of how well your children ski, and let them know what the limits are and what the penalties for exceeding them will be. But on balance, it's a good experience for them.

Finally, don't use a ski school as a warehouse for your kids so that you can go off skiing and "have fun." The worst problem children face in skiing is the feeling that Mom and Dad regard them as a drag. Use ski school for a valid purpose: teaching your child how to ski better, or correcting a specific fault you spot. Bob Kunkel comments that children have only two reasons for being in ski school, because they want to be or because they have to be, and of the two "want" is far better. Don't spoil school or learning for them. The most serious problem a child faces in skiing could be feeling unwanted and unable to share the fun with you.

Photo courtesy of Indianhead Mountain, Wakefield, Michigan.

"I met this one father who seemed like an awfully nice guy, except that right before the lesson began he turned to his son and said, 'I expect you to be skiing parallel by the end of the class.'"
BOB KUNKEL

"Don't 'overski' and frighten your child by taking him on a trail that's too tough for him, just because you want to have a good run."
BARBARA ROYLANCE

3

WHAT ADULT PROBLEMS MUST YOU SOLVE?

Whether you call it pressure, great expectations, or the "Little League Syndrome" we'll discuss in Part III, the biggest barriers to children's natural tendency to enjoy skiing are built by their parents. Parents can become preoccupied with "form" and a need for demonstrable progress from each lesson. Maybe those things are all right in the so-called adult world, but they louse things up for youngsters by robbing them of the experience of its *fun*.

Being a lawyer, I use that word "rob" accurately: to take (steal) by force or threat. Too often we forget how powerful a figure we are to our children, especially when they're young and dependent on us for survival and approval. They tend to accept our values; if we tell them they're skiing poorly if they aren't "parallel" almost as often as we *think* we are (check yourself on videotape sometime), they'll believe it. Racers are never parallel (except by accident), and the leading ski schools themselves aren't pushing "parallel" anymore as the "final form" for either kids or adults.

Why hang that kind of burden around your progeny's shoulders? Frankly, I wish I could enjoy skiing as much as Greg does, to ski with his total abandon and lack of concern about how he looks to others. I've tried to let him do things his way, and if I'm not overjoyed with how he's skiing or think I perceive a major flaw, I usually put him in ski school and let them make any necessary corrections. Then I discuss the results and diagnosis with the instructor after the class (preferably with Greg out of hearing range) and follow his advice. At least I try to do all that, but sometimes I snarl too.

Further, don't expect continual "progress," as we've mentioned before. Bob Kunkel tells of one youngster he had at Copper Mountain for a week "who never got out of the beginner's circle." But, Bob said, "that kid had the greatest time. He helped all the newcomers adjust to the beginner's circle, and when he came back the following year he had, somehow, somewhere in the interim, jumped ahead of some of the youngsters who'd been in his original class."

This, I have to admit, was a tough problem for me. In the first couple of seasons, I would feel, from time to time, that Greg wasn't getting any "better" (whatever that means), and as soon as I communicated that to him some of the joy would go out of his day even if he paid attention to what I was trying to show him. Finally, the year he turned eight, I resolved to leave him more to his own devices and, occasionally, try to create a game to make a point just as the good instructors do. That tends to work better for both of us, although I haven't been as good as I should be.

One problem we adults perceive, and that children don't see as a problem at all, is their natural tendency to race down the slope in as close to a straight line as humanly possible, deviating only if they see an interesting bump to jump over (to get to which they suddenly reveal previously hidden skills in making brilliant turns). In contrast, most adults feel that skiing should be a matter of linked, graceful, controlled turns. Parents can make this different orientation a contrast of wills, or we can reduce it to a more subtle game: "Bet you a Coke you can't make ten turns between here and that patch of ice," which he was about to make a beeline for anyway just to see what happened when he skied over it.

That game plan works both ways: Sometimes, when he says "race you to the top of that bump," you should go along with that. You have to check the trail to make sure you find a seam in the traffic, but you really can't cop out and expect him to play by your rules all the time. (Besides, the youngsters are right: Running straight *is* fun.)

This "game" thing can have its lighter and quite revealing moments. One beautiful spring day in 1980, the four of us were skiing down a gentle intermediate trail at Stratton, and it was Alix's turn to lead. My rule is that she make ten turns and then stop. Ordinarily, she would make those ten turns in about three and a half inches (or so it seemed), but she'd quietly been getting quite annoyed at doing that, since she really prefers to ski nonstop. This time when I gave her the ten-turn injunction, she proceeded to reveal a previously hidden talent for making long, wide, sweeping GS-type turns and got halfway down the slope while Dee and I stood up top and watched, mouths agape. "Where'd she learn that?" I asked Greg finally. He shrugged, as if the question were too silly and the answer too obvious to bother with. Then he took off and got to exactly the same spot making exactly the same ten turns.

One adult perception that must be transmitted to children is that of danger. Tom Montemagni of Mount Snow notes that one problem of putting kids on skis too young is that they lack the fear, and the accompanying sense of discretion, that tells an adult or older child when he's courting disaster. Youngsters up to maybe seven are apt to drop casually onto a wicked, steep, icy, tight, expert trail without adequate skills to handle it, and they do run into trees and other skiers. As a parent, you have *the* responsibility to keep your child off that type of terrain, and to teach him how to recognize it.

However, you can overdo this. I met a woman once who cheerfully admitted she escorted her children down the trail "in high C, shouting imprecations of doom at every turn." This seems to be more a maternal than paternal problem, and I suspect that her children, after they reached a certain age, turned her off and just skied. I try to shout warnings only when necessary and avoid the "boy-crying-wolf" syndrome. If I pick the terrain properly the problems will be minimal, and by explaining how I made the choice (and ignored other trails), I can increase their respect and apprehension levels. A *bit* of fear is a good trait.

Parents shouldn't become so concerned about the danger that they spoil the skiing for themselves and their children. Even if you inadvertently pick a wrong trail—and we've all done it—just talk your child down calmly, make frequent stops, and even suggest that you, too, are having problems. True, that's the toughest hangup of all to overcome—parental infallibility—but try. They really do know we're human.

Still, we have to realize we're human too, and no matter how much we discipline ourselves to follow the strictures in Chapter 7 (and elsewhere), sometimes you just have to let it hang out and *ski,* when you just cannot tolerate another run on Monotony Ridge. You can do this two ways: face up to and admit it (and find someone somehow to watch your child while you take that run or two), or bury it deep and justify skiing a tougher run by saying, "it's good for his soul to encounter this" or "he really can ski it." Barbara Roylance says that the latter is a no-no; don't push a young skier beyond what he feels he can ski, and, certainly, don't suddenly take off down that trail and tell him to follow you. Like Barbara, I've seen too much of that.

As I mentioned in the introduction, children who ski (or want to ski) sometimes face a totally different series of problems: parents who don't ski, or single parents who feel they can't take a child or children skiing by themselves. I think either pattern is a shame for both the children and the parents.

If you don't ski at all—and face it, the overwhelming majority of Americans, or people anywhere, don't—this doesn't mean your children can't. All across ski country, "from Portland to Portland," school groups and local ski areas have cooperative and effective ski-learning programs, sometimes during the afternoon (even early evening on night-skiing slopes) as part of physical education or "gym," and sometimes during the weekends on a less formal but more relaxed busing-based system. I can tell you that the ski areas I've discussed these programs with—usually the smaller or mid-sized areas—are quite dedicated to producing good skiers at very reasonable prices (sometimes as little as a dollar or two per session) because, as Dave Currier of Pat's Peak, New Hampshire, said, "Those are our customers of the future." This dedication is generally more pronounced at those areas regarded as a "local industry" by the natives, compared with the major national destination resorts, but as a rule, ski areas do a very good job in these programs.

Sometimes they do so good a job that your heir tries to entice you into skiing yourself or taking him on a ski vacation elsewhere. If you've developed a rational firsthand distaste for sliding down a frigid hill on two skinny pieces of plastic, feel free to say no; but if your decision is based on a belief that you're too old to learn to ski or that a ski vacation would bore you to tears, think again.

* *You're rarely too old to learn.* For all we pseudopurists tend to deplore it, the Graduated Length Method was designed with nonskiing adults in mind —and it works. People have started skiing in their fifties and older and become reasonably proficient at it; more important, they've learned to enjoy it, which is what it's all about. An awesome number of ski areas in all parts of the country do an excellent job in their learn-to-ski programs for adults of all ages. Not too long ago, covering the seventy-plus race at Hunter, New York, I met a man who didn't start skiing until well after he retired—and he now logs fifty days a season as he nears eighty. That same day, incidentally, more than thirty racers above the age of seventy got down the course, a few in better time than I'd have managed and at least a dozen in comparable time. I strongly suggest that no matter how old you are, you'd better get your legs and wind into some kind of condition—but you don't have to be ready to run the Boston Marathon.

* *Ski resorts can be fun even if you don't ski.* Some, anyway. While few besides Aspen and Vail, Colorado, have a sufficient variety of nonskiing activities to entertain a nonskier for a full week, dozens of other resorts offer enough activity to provide a pleasant weekend while the children ski. I've even met many nonskiing parents who truly enjoy sitting in base lodges watching the color and action (although I must admit it baffles me), but my own preference would be to select a resort whose satellite experiences and pastimes appeal to you: ice-skating, tennis, shopping, even gambling (Lake Tahoe has some of the best skiing in the United States nearby). As an alternative, many major resorts run large conferences and conventions on a wide range of topics aimed at a vast array of industries (medical, real estate, writing, etc.); if you attend one, why not take your child skiing with you? Conversely, why not check to see if any ski resorts are running conventions or seminars you'd be interested in attending during a school holiday? Many resorts also have good to excellent restaurants, and some have traveling theatrical or musical groups passing through.

* *Ski areas can care for children of all ages.* This is important both for parents who don't ski and for single parents who do (or want to learn). Of much interest, Mount Snow linked its involvement in the all-day SKIwee program for youngsters up to twelve (see Part IV) to adult participation in a program called "Parents Who Ski." Vail (other majors are following suit) and many small areas have well-developed all-day programs for teenagers as well, from rank beginner to junior racer. While I personally feel a single parent should spend some time skiing with his children on vacation, these programs safely allow you to learn how to ski without worrying about whether your child is safe and/or having fun.

I have, in fact, only one caveat for the nonskiing or single parent: Beware, skiing is addictive, and you can get hooked into the inner circle at some of the smaller ski areas. The big danger is the small-time racing circuit (see Chapter 16), because the junior programs always need volunteers—gatekeepers, starters, program directors, chauffeurs, etc.—and often offer a discount on the price if you "pitch in." Far worse, most skiers are very nice people, and once you get drawn into the "second-floor kaffeeklatch" where the racing people hang out, it's tough to leave. Worst of all, you won't want to.

"*Kids need the advantage of peer pressure they get in a skiweek. They're used to playing, learning, and moving in a group from regular school.*"
TOM MONTEMAGNI

"*Children learn best through repetition, several days of short lessons in a row.*"
PAM STENMARK,
Seminar Center, Vail

"*The novice knows he doesn't have to learn it all in one day. He's more patient with himself.*"
BOB KUNKEL

"*The Saturday-morning lesson is a waste of time and money.*"
GARY ANDRUS
former marketing director, Copper Mountain
(the quoting of which drew the ire
of two of my panel of experts)

4

WHY SHOULD YOU START WITH A SKIWEEK?

While I rarely give credence to those marketing-inspired blurbs that appear in ski-area brochures (and some of my best friends write them), every so often someone comes up with a statement of value where the seller's and buyer's truths overlap and the pitch is valid. This is the case when you confront that most intricate of all questions: Should you start your child's skiing career with a skiweek, a weekend, or a one-day venture?

Believe it, the skiweek has it all over the other two options:

* The tensions and hassles are reduced.

* The strangeness vanishes.

* The skiweek programs are designed and integrated better.

* Peer pressure works for you.

* Children can seek a more natural learning pace.

As we mentioned in Chapter 2, city and suburban children face an awesome problem the first time they visit a ski area: the strangeness of the experience. You probably had the same initial reaction—I did—but we adults have a lot of experience coping with alien situations. Children don't. You can cope. They can't. You expect them to cope. They don't. Crisis.

Consider the situation if you choose to launch your child's ski career on a busy Saturday morning. Unless you have mastered Chapter 6, on how to plan a ski day, the chances of your getting to Mount Zilch before 9 A.M. are nil. Odds are heavy that you forgot to rent your child's equipment before you got to the area and that you haven't the foggiest idea where either the rental shop, ski-school desk, or class-meeting place is. When you get to the area, you see hundreds of other anxious people milling around the overworked rental shop, the frantic ski-school desk, and the chaotic meeting place. The one overriding emotion you feel is frustration: *You* want to be out there skiing. You didn't drive two, four, or six hours to race from place to place, only to learn you just missed getting your child into that beginners' class (for which you've already paid last week's wages) because you didn't hook him into those strange, rented skisbootsbindingspoles (for which you paid the prior week's wages) in time. So you and your beloved spouse, assuming he/she has the same desire to ski you do, argue over who gets stuck with schlepping your child around the snow at the base for an hour while the other skis. (If I sound like I've been there . . .)

All your child knows about this mess is that you've been very tense for an hour or more and that, somehow, he was the reason. Since the last thing he wants to do is make you angry, he feels hostile toward this skiing thing that caused it all.

Or, assume you were a bit luckier/smarter/earlier and got everything together in time to launch him in that beginner class. He hasn't had time to acclimate to the area and the experience before you *abandon* him to this alien world with its strange teachers telling him to do odd things with those weird gizmos on his feet and surrounded by children he doesn't know. Just so that you can go off skiing by yourself.

Finally, this session ends, and, assuming you watch the time, don't try for that "extra run," and know where to gather him up, you've got him for the rest of the day—at which time you parents argue over who gets to schlepp him around.

Also, the collection-at-ski-school time coincides with the time most people quit for lunch, the time we veterans eschew the lunchroom as if it were serving the plague. (This isn't an editorial comment on the quality of the food.) It's true, some of us have been known to toss a five-spot at our spouse, mutter, "Why don't you and Greg have lunch now, I'm not really hungry anyway," and then split quickly for the lifts. The impolite dialogue about this move in the car going home further convinces a youngster that skiing is like anchovies and vegetables and wine: a weird thing that adults enjoy but about which intelligent human animals like children know better.

All in all, a Saturday at Mount Zilch is a zilch as his first skiing experience.

In contrast, a skiweek can be a laid-back, loosy-goosy, happy experience if you plan it correctly and understand how the schedule works *for* you. The learn-to part usually occupies only five of the nine days, Monday to Friday, although many resorts' programs are longer. Depending on your travel schedule, you'll probably get to the resort Friday night or early Saturday, which at first seems to repeat the Saturday fiasco at Mount Zilch. It doesn't have to. Instead, you can take it easy that first day: Show him around the area—lodge, lifts, bathrooms, lunchroom, ski-school section, ski-patrol room—and let him acclimate to the *feel* of the situation. Sure, you and your spouse can each take a few runs during the day, but knock off early, take your child to the rental shop during the afternoon to get his equipment for the week, then let him put it on and try a few tentative steps. On Sunday, put him in the nursery in the morning while you ski, meet him for lunch, then take turns "skiing" with him in alternate hour-long bursts. By now, he'll be somewhat familiar with his equipment, a big plus when he enters ski school the following morning.

Most of the better resorts have learn-to-skiweek orientation programs scheduled sometime Sunday afternoon or evening, accompanied by films and talks and cocktail parties (Cokes for the kids). Your child will probably meet some children he'll be with in class, and those familiar faces, in a now-familiar environment, will make Monday morning a lot more comfortable —to the point where he'll probably be happy to see you ski away, if he even notices!

We could discuss the pros and cons of half- versus full-day lesson programs for hours without drawing any conclusion. As a teaching/learning method, full-day is unquestionably superior. It allows for a cohesiveness of teaching progression and adapts to the short, intensive attention span of young children in particular, but, I have to tell you, both of my children hate them with a passion and prefer (a mild word) to ski at least half the day with us. But either half- or full-day, a skiweek program lets both you and your child relax and play with skiing, because you shouldn't feel that need to nurse every last second of straight-out skiing from an eight-day skiweek, compared with a Saturday-only situation.

The skiweek has still another advantage. Even at the best ski resorts—I have to agree with Andrus, based on my experiences —the ninety-minute Saturday-morning lesson tends to be a waste of time even for experienced skiers and teachers. Instructors aren't to blame so much as chaotic conditions resulting from latecomers, equipment problems, and the like. The result is poor compared with a skiweek class.

In addition, those well-conceived progressions designed for skiweek classes tend to disintegrate on Saturday—a point made best by Dave Chapman, director of the Pat's Peak, New Hampshire, ski school, who feels that these programs are designed by PSIA to serve the needs of the big resorts and don't consider the problem of the weekend/day area. That could be, but whatever the reason, it's pretty tough to put together a string of lessons—a progression—over a series of one-shot weekend lessons. It's true, as Montemagni and Stenmark note, that the weekend, part-time instructor is apt to be every bit as good as the full-timer—and often more enthusiastic—and it's equally true that a good instructor can give "even a busload of skiers a good lesson" on a Saturday, as Montemagni notes. But no one will dispute that a weeklong, day-after-day program will teach someone how to ski faster and better on a more integrated basis. (Tom adds, incidentally, that if you do pursue the weekend route, take either an all-day or an *afternoon* lesson. Good advice.)

The advantages of the skiweek are that the instructors can weigh and watch the children carefully, move them up and down in classes as needed, and spot and work on specific problem areas. The programs often have the personnel to assign one instructor to one or two children for much of the morning or day. By the end of Tuesday every child has a name, a personality, and a prognosis, and by Thursday or Friday they can ski.

At the beginning of the chapter I mentioned "peer pressure," which I'm sure isn't exactly strange to you if any of your children are in school or a play group. The skiweek group, especially in the hands of a competent instructor, becomes close-knit and, therefore, effective. If you assume, as I do, that kids *learn* rather than *are taught,* this peer group makes them want to learn; and assuming the ski school groups and regroups the classes to keep their ability and performance levels close, the "singleness of purpose, the common triumphs and failures" help to push them ahead quickly, according to Montemagni.

How quickly? By that second Saturday, you'll be able to ski with your child—which will move you to Chapter 7.

I must conclude with an admission: Until February 1980 I'd never put Greg or Alix into a full skiweek program because my assignments rarely let me spend even three, much less five, days in a row at one area. I still haven't managed five, but in order to check out how well SKIwee (see Part IV) was working in its maiden season, we logged three days at Waterville Valley. For the first time, both Greg and Alix were willing to spend the whole day away from us without complaint (although Greg managed to hustle "just one more run" with me every afternoon), and both showed an incredible amount of improvement. They also liked the luxury of staying in a condo near the slopes and eating out every night— compared with the regimen of Chapter 6 —and no question, it worked well.

Even before that, Greg and Alix improved faster during vacations, skiing eight or nine days in a row, than in a comparable number of one- or two-day bursts during weekends. Also, I progressed more in a five-day advanced-skiing workshop at Sugarbush than in whole fifty-day seasons in which I've received almost uncountable ad hoc private lessons from some of the top ski-school directors in the country.

I have no doubts that the best way for anyone, child or adult, to learn how to ski is in a skiweek. If you can't schedule it, make do the best you can on day lessons (see Chapter 6); but try to work it out.

Photo courtesy of Keystone, Colorado.

"Isn't it nice skiing one area all the time where you can make friends and your kids are all in the same racing program?"
LONGTIME VETERAN
at Pat's Peak

"I get tired of skiing even Vail all of the time."
A GOOD FRIEND OF MINE
in Denver

"A season's pass lets you justify spending the extra money to rent a locker for the season—and isn't that nice!"
TOM MONTEMAGNI

5

HOW SHOULD YOU PLAN A SKI SEASON?

My parents' generation was very big on the "we're doing it for the kids" routine, but I must admit that my reaction was alternately resentment and disbelief. When it comes to planning a ski season, and despite all the emphasis this book places on children's happiness and welfare, let me say one thing flat out: Think of yourself first.

If you don't, you're going to have a rotten season, and you'll lay that burden on the kids, and then they'll have a lousy season. If you're a strong and serious skier, you won't be able to tolerate twenty-five days on a 500-foot burial mound with six trails ranging from flat to boring. If you need a big mountain, go for it—even if it costs a few (or many) bucks more—because then you'll be "up" for the season, and so will the rest of the family. (Well, we'll talk about that in the next chapter.)

Planning a ski season, especially with youngsters, takes some serious planning. You have to consider the ski-school programs and the other things children need, and weave all that into your requirements. This demands a change in all our thinking. Until Greg arrived, my wife and I never thought about the season until the day it began—defined as the first day we headed north —and we played it loose until the day we put away the hardware. But since Greg and Alix expanded our family, we've begun to plan most of the season as soon as we get the school vacation calendar. Those happy-go-lucky, play-it-by-ear days are gone forever, or at least until Greg and Alix are old enough to go off by themselves, but we manage to have as good a season as we ever did.

Those admonitions "Think of yourself first" versus "You have to plan for the kids" aren't a contradiction. You have two levels of planning and decision-making: objective and subjective. The first involves the numbers, as in dollars; the second focuses on you, as in likes and dislikes.

On the first, accept as gospel that you have to make an early decision on whether to go the season-pass route. If you do, make a list of the areas in your regular skiing region, check with other parents to see which areas have good children's ski-school programs, write for the brochures, and compare the rates for a family of your size. Include the cost of children's ski-school programs. Then, assuming your region spans several sub-regions, such as the Catskills, the Berkshires, and southern Vermont for New York City, compare the relative costs of housing and transportation; season rentals and gasoline are expensive. The results will eliminate many of the original contenders and produce, on paper, a clear winner or two.

This brings you to the subjective: "But I don't wanna spend the whole season at that bump with those creeps." Fair enough. Move up the price line until you find one you can live with. Then consult with the other adult member of the family, who may prefer something with more intermediate terrain, and negotiate. Now you're in business.

The reason I said to start planning early is because (1) Mom and Dad occasionally "discuss" that Mount A versus Mount B bit at some length, and (2) ski areas have definite season-pass cutoff dates, after which the prices increase until, ultimately, they disappear. So do house and/or condominium rentals.

For most serious-skiing families, the season pass is the only decision that makes sense. Although rates vary widely among areas, depending on region, state, relative size of the area, ages and size of the family, as a quick rule a single adult will need twenty-five days of skiing to "earn" his season pass but a family of four will break even (against single-day ticket rates) between ten and fifteen days. However, that season-pass suggestion is based on a few assumptions: You plan to ski more than ten days a season, money is a consideration, and the competence of the children's ski school is among your concerns. Let's refine this:

* *How much do you ski?* Assuming you break the ten-day barrier, do you log fifteen? twenty-five? forty days? Do you go every weekend plus one or two weeks of vacation? If you ski often and well, you may find it interesting to find a large area whose pass is interchangeable with another area; Mount Snow's pass, for instance, can be used at Killington and Sunday River, Maine, for a small surcharge. Waterville Valley now owns and manages Bobcat/Crotched. You'll still key on one area for the ski-school schedule, but you can bounce on other days.

* *How primitive a base set-up will you tolerate?* Every year or so, in one guise or another, *SKI* magazine does an obligatory article on those still-remaining-primitive-but-lovely-places-where-you-can-ski-for-38-cents-with-a-free-lesson-and-lunch-tossed-in, and the story is the biggest waste of space, time, paper, and ink, not to mention postage, of the season. Advertisers demand a rerun if they're placed next to it. Fact is, no one goes to those cutesy-primitive-but-cheap areas unless he's dirt poor, a relative of the owner, or a rank beginner, because the satellite services at these areas are inadequate, and, all too often, so is the maintenance. The more you ski an area, the more these backup facilities become important—especially the bar for those days when only addicts take more than two runs—because they'll define the other people who'll ski the area and with whom you'll strike up a season-long friendship. So pick an area you'll be happy with, because the other "regulars" will probably be people you'll be happy knowing, and your children will probably like theirs.

  * *How good should the ski-school program be?* Part IV
    goes into detail on this, but let me offer here one
    other major cautionary about season passes. People
    tend to get a mite casual about using them on mar-
    ginal days (minus-40° windchills, gray overcast, ice
    on the road, and such), especially if one of the adults
    is a "fair-weather skier." Don't yield to the tempta-
    tion; this is the day when those drills mentioned in
    the next chapter provide the necessary discipline to
    get the youngsters to ski school on time. The subtle
    reason for this discipline is to get the youngsters used
    to skiing comfortably on those less-than-perfect days.
    Obviously, you have to worry about frostbite and
    similar problems, but aside from that, let them learn
    how to ski on ice and in crud, in a snowstorm and in
    flat light. That's a large part of what skiing's about,
    playing with nature in all its moods, and the children
    are going to take their cue from you; if you chicken
    out, so will they.

Another advantage of buying a season pass is that you may
be able to avoid most of the pitfalls and hassles mentioned in
the next chapter by renting a locker in which you can stow your
equipment (rather than schlepping it back and forth every day)
and, at those areas where you get permanent passes you can use
on liftlines, avoid waiting on line to get lift tickets and ski-
school tickets. A season pass also gives your children instant
identification cards if they're injured when you're not skiing
with them.

Another facet of planning the season is equipment (see Part II).
My injunction against buying hardware at a ski-area shop
vanishes if you have a season pass. In fact, it might even be
worth paying the extra few bucks to buy your equipment from
that area's shop compared with a city shop, because if anything
goes wrong with a piece of hardware, you're right where you

bought it. Also, that shop is quite apt to give your needs—tuning, repairs, etc.—higher priority in a crunch if it made the sale in the first place. This is especially vital with boots, where proper fitting these days is such a drawn-out process.

Either way, ski area or city/town shop, do your buying early. September or October. Children's equipment moves especially fast; in mid-October 1979, I bought Alix the last pair of mittens my regular shop had in her size. Everything else was on reorder. Selections in clothing dwindle well before Thanksgiving. Some equipment companies give junior items second priority in the early manufacturing and/or shipping runs, and you may face a delay getting a Jaguar or a Tyrolia 30 or a Garmont if you wait until late in November. (Also, remember to hit those big sales in March for items you can safely use next season.)

My usual admonition to adults—wait until your feet shrink back to winter size before buying boots—doesn't hold for children. Given the fact that their feet grow expensively in the course of a ski boot's life, buying boots in September when they have fat feet might be a smart move.

Buying early also gives the shop time to mount bindings, prepare the bottoms, and engrave your children's names properly, compared with that usual November crush where the backshop has a zillion pairs to mount for yesterday. Even in my "off seasons" when I'm not buying any new hardware, I give my equipment to the shop in mid-October to get ready for the season.

Finally, set up a regular schedule for tuning skis and checking bindings. Kids' equipment, if anything, needs attention more often than yours. Learn each shop's rhythm and 'druthers: Some are set up to handle a Saturday overnight, others prefer a Sunday night/Saturday morning spread. Also, to forestall delay in getting your equipment back in the morning, arrange for a rapid pickup either by prepaying or establishing credit.

Planning doesn't end with season pass and equipment. Equally important are logistics—housing and transportation—and I strongly suggest you make your decisions in September, as soon as you get your school calendar. If you opt for a season pass, try to rent a house or condo on the mountain if your budget can carry it, assuming the area has some. However, if you must use your car to get to the area, you might as well locate ten or fifteen miles away (rather than two or three) and save the money on the rental. Another option is to locate in a town central to four or more areas—Weston, Vermont, or Frisco, Colorado, for example—where you'll probably pay less and gain freedom of opportunity. The rule here, as with season passes, is to shop around, weigh the trade-offs, and sign your lease as soon as you buy your passes.

For my money, if you're dedicated to skiing and plan to remain with it a while, buying rather than renting a house or condo is far the smarter move. We did this more than a decade ago and have never regretted the decision. But do your homework; this is a real-estate, not a skiing, decision, and investment opportunities are tricky.

Equally important, learn the *winter* range of your car: How many miles will it travel comfortably on a full tank wearing snow tires, carrying a full load of people, and using heater/defroster and other systems? (A helpful tip: Remove your ski rack between weekend trips, since it decreases mileage by 10 to 15 percent.) If your house is more than a tankful away, learn where the gas stations are, which ones remain open late, and how late, and plan your regular schedule so that you leave early enough to refill. I refill anyway, even though my ski house is within a tankful's range of home, because (1) I like the weight of the extra gas when I hit the backroads, (2) I don't trust any car or brand of gas completely, and (3) I hate to waste the time filling up on Saturday morning. These days, this kind of caution isn't excessive.

One last thing: You'll want to know how to plan and hedge against the possibility that it won't snow that season. Simple. You can't.

Bromley Mountain, Vermont. Photo courtesy of Vermont Ski Area News Bureau.

"*Some days, we get to the area by eleven A.M., but on other days, things don't go so well.*"

ANONYMOUS
(lest I lose a friend)

6

HOW SHOULD YOU PLAN
A SKI DAY?

We have these friends who have escalated the challenge of getting a family of four to a ski area from a problem to absolute chaos, involving two cars, three lost hours, and at least four major confrontations. Somehow, of late, they manage to log about five days of skiing in a season—all the more amazing because these people bought a second home near a major ski resort several years ago to reduce the crisis. I have to wonder what the tumult and trouble is all about, because it isn't all that difficult.

Our "ski house" is roughly an hour from almost any place we ski, and two hours from some of our favorite areas, yet we rarely reach the parking lot after 9 A.M. We are, no matter what my wife says, highly organized in our approach.

The alarm goes off ninety minutes before the car launch (determined the night before), and my wife is propelled from the bed immediately (if not always willingly). My job is to dress me, which is rather easy, and the kids, which gets progressively easier year by year. On Saturdays, I mount the skirack, get the skis locked on, and make sure the car starts and is ready to pull away at the appointed time. In the interim, my wife makes breakfast and lunch (we're inveterate brown-baggers), gets herself dressed (which is rarely easy), wastes valuable time cleaning the house, and off we go. On time. Kids in tow.

Sounds simple, yes? It hasn't always been. Getting this act together takes discipline, devotion, concentration, attention to detail, and an absolute imperviousness to muttered distaff complaints like, "But it's twenty-two below and *raining*" (which, as we New Hampshire-types know, isn't quite as impossible as it seems on January weekends). The reason we make it work is quite simple: We believe it's worth the effort. No matter what my wife says a couple of mornings every season.

What delays most people is what a friend of mine calls the people-quantum theory, which means adding half an hour for each extra person you're taking anyplace. When I'm skiing alone I need less than half an hour from wake-up to drive-off, and far less if I plan to hit the Egg-McMuffin-to-go route. When Greg and I are skiing we need almost an hour. The whole family needs almost two. This theorum works, and, despite three years of serious, concentrated study, shepherding, and salesmanship, I have been unable to reduce it below ninety minutes. Sometimes I make breakfast, and occasionally we buy lunch. I don't always win the battles, but we always drive off on time. If you lose it there, you've lost the day. Believe it. That's the key.

Planning a ski day takes consultation, coordination, cooperation, establishing sequence and priorities, and, occasionally, brute force.

The first decision to be made is: Where are we going? (If you have a season pass, move to square two.) This affects two things: What time we are leaving (which determines when we're getting up), and which way I will turn as I leave my driveway. (Left we go to Vermont, right we stay in New Hampshire.) This decision must be made the night before.

The second question is: Are the children going to ski school that day? This definitely must be decided the night before, because that means we *really* have to be there by 9. (So, we backslide now and then.)

The third question is: Are we eating dinner home or at a restaurant that night? This also must be decided the night before, because it affects the cargo to be packed into the knapsacks or car trunk. No one, least of all youngsters, should be forced to eat dinner wearing long johns and bib overalls, so jeans become part of the materiel accompanying the marching orders.

With those decisions made, we have most of the problem licked.

Since morning in our household tends to be awful under the most optimum of conditions, I must have everything arranged the night before. Specifically:

* Knapsacks are packed and stacked at Position A near the door. As soon as we get home at night, all wet items are removed and replaced. Boots that need work are fixed immediately and repacked, and the bags placed in the same location every night. If I seem insistent about that, it's because I once left Alix's boot-bag home, which was a very silly—not to mention time-consuming—thing to do. Never again!?

* The first night of every trip (weekend or full week), the skis and poles are stacked in Position B, with the skirack leaning against the door. From then on until the end of the trip, the skis remain locked on the car (I'm insured). If it rains, we remove them, dry the edges and bindings, and stack them again at Position B.

* Clothing for the children is selected and piled, in order of installation, at the foot of their respective beds. My wife and I usually eschew doing this for ourselves because we can, at least nine days out of ten, make these decisions in reasonable time in the morning.

* Decide *before* the first day of the season who's responsible for carrying what from house to car and from the parking lot to the base lodge; stick to it, but be reasonable: A five-year-old cannot carry skis, boots, and poles more than ten feet. An eight-year-old can, provided *you* have put the handling package together

properly. Get a skirack that can carry a pair of skis
locked into a Ski Tote (few can also handle locked
poles), and under no conditions consider a rack on
which you have to split a pair of skis; locking them
together again in the lot, by brake or leash, wastes
time. Make sure the children's knapsacks fit comfortably and won't slip off. In other words, don't fumble on
the ten-yard line.

Okay, now you're there. On time. All equipment in place.
You got it licked, right? Wrong. You're not skiing yet. It's
first-and-goal on the five, but you still have tickets to buy if
you don't have a season pass, boots and software to put on,
classes to meet or tots to put into the nursery. Our procedure
is to lock the skis onto a rail outside, then have my wife take
care of buckling their boots while I get tickets and coffee and
hot chocolate, but I'm still never the last to buckle up and go.
When you really get your act together, you can get from car
to chairlift in fifteen or twenty minutes, while if you lose it
here you can lose an hour.

Now, some of this may sound excessive, but remember that
the youngsters often have a vested interest in stalling: Being late
means they don't have to go to ski school. Remember also that
even experienced young skiers haven't got boot-buckling down
to that automatic tightening sequence adults do, and that they
have to *think* about putting on dickeys, hats, mittens, and
goggles.

Sometimes I feel that planning and executing all details of a
ski day, from getting up to getting home, makes Patton's
turning the Third Army up to the Bulge look like child's play.
I've spent six chapters talking about it, and we still haven't hit
the liftline, much less considered some other little problems,
such as:

* Getting the youngsters *into* school and/or nursery.

* Getting them *from* school and/or nursery.

* Getting lunch from the car to the base lodge to coincide with the arrival of the kids from school and/or nursery, not to mention finding space to sit and eat same in the little cellar room reserved for brown-baggers (which room and rule I tend to ignore anyway).

* Deciding who's skiing with whom when, where, and for how long.

* Deciding on a time and place for all contingents to meet after skiing.

* Making sure the kids have identification and Ski Tote lock numbers someplace safe (but not so safe they can't find them).

Plus . . . Enough already. Let's end this section with a chapter about *skiing*.

*"I like to hold little kids between my knees
and ski them down the slope."*
I. WILLIAM BERRY

"That's absolutely the worst thing you can do!"
JUDY REISS,
director of the Valley Day School, Sugarbush

"I've always preferred the leash."
JOHN BURROWS,
former marketing director at Loon Mountain

*"Try skiing backward bending over
holding their tips together."*
PAM STENMARK
(Sure, Pam.)

*"If you ski alongside them
and let them hold your
poles . . ."*
CHRISTI NORTHROP,
SKIwee coordinator

*"I like to hold little kids between my knees
and ski them down the slope."*
ME

7

HOW DO YOU SKI
WITH YOUNG BEGINNERS?

There is, alas, no universally accepted system on how parents should take little ones down the slope early in their careers. While the pros tend to decry the between-the-knees technique, neither of my little skiers seems to have suffered any irremediable damage from the experience. Of all the other techniques, I guess that Pam's is about the best, but for one minor problem: I can't ski backwards very well, much less bending over holding a kid's skitips. I like the holding-the-skipoles (points toward *you*) technique as the second stage, when they've gotten tired of between-the-knees and are getting adventurous. I have philosophic objections to togging a kid out with a leash, but John definitely made it work with his son. I guess that if I had to offer a conclusion it's simply this: Do whatever works for you.

The main objections offered to between-the-knees are twofold: (1) the children become too dependent on you, and (2) they don't stand on their skis, preferring to keep most of their weight on the crossed poles (my method) or to lean back against you if you eschew the poles and just hold them. (I can add a third objection: "My thighs hurt.") Both complaints are potentially valid, if you let the kids get away with either. What I have found, especially covering the second objection, is that you can slowly get your child to stand on his skis as he logs more snowtime and develops more confidence; you feel his weight lessen on the poles as he begins to stand higher. All it takes is patience. Both of my children showed a distinct desire not to become overly dependent; in fact, they couldn't wait to get out and fly on their own.

All it takes is patience, or, as my wife used to say, "Remember, some day it will all be worth it." (How quickly she forgot —but that's another story.) It is worth it. All it takes . . .

Skiing with little kids—one and a half to three or four—is a lot of fun. It takes some understanding and a bit of compassion, and it really doesn't hurt the operation if you know something about skiing (although that's not nearly as important as your feeling confident).

Children are frightened the first few times they're on the snow (we discuss that nonsense about children having no fear in Part IV). It's alien. They're not used to sliding. They're probably cold. They're not used to seeing you in that clothing or being surrounded by all those other people. If they come from city or suburb they're not used to a mountain. So the first job is to get them used to sliding on snow and feeling comfortable outdoors.

Admittedly, this won't be the most exciting moment you've ever spent on skis; walking around on the flat holding your child's hand doesn't quite compare with blowing it out on High Rustler. Equally annoying, you'll probably spend more time strapping those plastic skis onto his boots, then restrapping them, then strapping them again, than you will actually spend sliding. But just keep telling yourself, this too shall pass.

It will. By the second or third day, you start playing "catch" —also known as go-ski-to-Mommy, or why-do-I-always-have-to-schlepp-him-up-the-hill? On this last item, the best uphill transportation method those first days is to tuck him under one arm as you climb (the human-chairlift technique). The next stage is to anthropomorphize into the human T-bar, where you have him hold the handle end of the pole as you climb, or into a Poma-lift, where you slip the pole baskets between his legs and pull, which Pam Stenmark prefers. Then you graduate to where you put a hand on his backside and push as you climb; one thing you do a lot of in those early sessions is climb. (It won't do you any harm.) The farther along that progression you go, the higher you climb, and you continue to hope that Mommy's a good catcher. What amazes you most is how quickly he learns to balance on those short squatty skis and slide, and even to turn to get to Mommy. You can even plant a pole and have him turn around it in a short time.

A good device, if that beginner is your younger child, is to have big brother help. (Just don't lose your sense of humor as they go tumbling over each other in the snow.) This is especially valuable if the youngest is one of those I-ain't-takin'-nothing-from-big-brother types; frankly, I suspect that Greg had more to do with Alix's early ski development than Mount Snow, Waterville Valley, Pat's Peak, my wife, and me all rolled into one. If you'd ever watched Alix's eyes watching him cruise arrogantly down the beginner slope you'd know what I mean.

Ultimately, you reach that day when you stop being the lift and start using those the area provides. First rule: Fight your instinct and ignore the T-bar unless you have thighs of steel, because transporting a short, uncertain kid on a surface lift is, to put it mildly, painful. (And I'm usually in pretty good shape.) Far better are chairlifts built close to the ground—the relics at Mount Snow may be the best ever for toddlers—because children do get apprehensive hanging thirty feet up in the air. My method for loading a small child is simple: I tuck him under my arm two people before I'm about to load, clomp on and sit down, wait till the chair stops swinging, sit him next to me, and hold him around the waist all the way up; shortly before it's time to unload I lift him back onto my lap and, depending on the height of the chair vis-a-vis the unloading ramp, either carry him off or let him slide off on his skis. (I also put the safety bar down as soon as possible and drill that into him right from ride one.) Most little children love that first ride, but some of the older ones get a bit nervous.

Now you face a tense and crucial moment: For the first time, that child can't see the bottom of the slope, or can see it and realizes it's a lot longer than anything he's ever done before.

The first few times, when he was three and four, Greg got frightened; Alix was more casual, having watched Greg handle it. That's when—no matter what Judy Reiss says—it's a big plus to put a young child between your knees to reassure him on that first run. I also kept talking to him, saying things like "whee" when we'd pick up a bit of speed, and "turn" when we did that (to implant that thought as early as possible, futile though it seems later), and consistently, "Isn't this fun?!" (This pays unexpected dividends. At five and a half, when she was skiing quite credibly, Alix suddenly confronted a short-but-steep-for-her mogul field at Mount Snow and asked if I'd take her down between my knees. I did. The next weekend she handled that field easily by herself without so much as a blink of hesitation.)

I think I prefer some of the smaller areas for these early voyages. Areas like Butternut Basin, Massachusetts, and Pat's Peak, New Hampshire, have some beautiful beginner trails where, as early as the third day of riding lifts, you can let a small child ski by himself on shallow slopes, either solo or holding your poles. Excellent beginner slopes at the big areas like Mount Snow can get crowded, and can scare a little child.

Small children have no endurance. Two runs on the beginner slope and it's back in for the hot chocolate. Accept it, live with it, don't begrudge it; you'll be surprised at how quickly that endurance grows, especially if you let them have fun and don't lay a subliminal look-what-I'm-giving-up-for-you rap on them.

The problem is, and let's not kid each other, you are giving up part of your ski day, and at today's prices that's nothing to laugh at. The question becomes immediately clear: How do you ski enough for yourself to justify going skiing? Our solution was to put Greg (later Alix) in the nursery until lunch, ski hard for three hours, then have lunch and take him out to ski. From time to time, as he got tired or cold, one of us would take him inside while the other took a few runs. Then we got back together on the beginner slope and repeated the process. We logged a fair amount of skiing this way, far more than when we followed the *apparently* smarter move and skied with Greg or Alix during the morning and got an afternoon-only ticket for ourselves. Take that on faith; I've clocked both routes.

At this point—after a few days of straight runs on a shallow slope—your child is ready for ski school. However, I must warn you: If you think you can now go off and log some real skiing for yourself, forget it. If anything, you'll have less time, because that earlier 9-to-noon free-skiing run suddenly becomes 10-to-noon (if you're lucky), and one of you has to be at the school at either end. Then, after lunch (which suddenly shrinks to three minutes and five seconds), he wants to show you what he learned in class and becomes willing to stay out longer. After several lessons, he can ski well enough so that you adults can alternate in skiing with him. Finally, he gets good enough to keep up with you, and that's real fun—until he gets too good, of course.

Remember, at this early stage of his skiing, praise is the key word. Don't try to correct or chastise, no matter what your instinct is. Worry later about technique; confidence is far more important after those initial lessons, and your constantly saying "good" boosts his morale.

A good skill for parents to learn is the shepherd-dog technique, especially with beginners flying on their own the first few times. Working on the theory that you're faster, quicker, and stronger than a six-year-old novice, you can ski either alongside or slightly behind, and accelerate to intercept a threat (another skier or lift-tower), then place your boot/ski alongside your child's boot/ski and either force a turn or lean down and lift him up.

From here on in, no matter what the age, they aren't little kids anymore, they're little skiers. You're at the point where you can put them into ski school for the whole day and really go off and wail on your own (at least, so the more competent parents tell me; I've flunked this).

Until, of course, it's time to take the next child through the sequence.

Part II

Clothing and Equipment

INTRODUCTION

I'm amazed at what parents often do to their children—parents who, just by their interest in skiing, suggest they're intelligent, affluent, and aggressive. If the demographics developed by the major magazines and consultants are at all accurate, the average skier has completed college (and often a professional or graduate school), earns at least $35,000 a year, has a second home, takes frequent vacations, eats at first-line restaurants, drinks the finest liquor, and so on. Yet you know how he often uses that intelligence, affluence, and good taste?

He looks to save $25 on his children's ski equipment and clothing. "That," says Norm Sweeney of Norm's Ski Shop in Keene, New Hampshire, "is what they'll pay for one Saturday-night dinner at Vail or Sugarbush, without even thinking about it, yet *saving* that twenty-five dollars will produce two seasons of discomfort for one of their children." Go figure it.

In defense of parents (being one, after all), I must admit that until about five years ago this penurious reaction was somewhat justified; the most painstaking investigations turned up junk no matter what the price was. Nobody was building good equipment or designing decent clothing for young skiers. The boots (except for one brand) were rubberized travesties, the bindings were deathtraps, the mittens were blotters, and the parkas were either so thin that even an adult would shiver or so bulky that the kid couldn't move. One reasonably good ski and one rigid two-by-four existed. We all despaired.

However, those days are over and, hopefully, parental reluctance to spend some time and a few bucks seeking good clothing and equipment is also history. Ski-school youth-program directors note a solid improvement in hardware and software the past year or two, and the better ski-shop owners (still a minority) are educating the parents they service about these improvements. Yet for all that, as I swept through a huge range of ski areas across the nation two years ago surveying programs and equipment, I still saw an awesome preponderance of junk and a high ratio of unhappy children. This must end, because the old alibi has vanished. Today, you've got good equipment and clothing.

How radical and rapid has this progress been?

* Throughout the 1970s, the boot choice was limited to Nordica, until Garmont started to move in 1977–78. Yet at the major manufacturers' show in Las Vegas in March 1979, the range had swollen to five: Caber, Dolomite, Dynafit, Garmont, and Nordica, with the last named having been forced to redesign its entire children's line just to keep pace with the new, hot competition. By 1981–82, even this lineup had changed, with Raichle moving up quickly into the top ranks and Garmont, via Italian bankruptcy (I think I'll leave that one alone), dropping out. Trappeur keeps promising but not quite delivering in the children's market, while Dachstein is beginning to emerge and Lange is finally producing a boot flexible by someone weaker than an elephant.

* In step-in bindings, Look and Salomon had dominated through the decade with (being generous) barely adequate models, until the Tyrolia 50 took command in 1977. At the 1979 Vegas show, Tyrolia's new three-model line (30–60–160) proved that kids, too, can be safely tied to a ski, finally forcing Salomon to scrap that old 101 in favor of two new 127 models that went into serious production for 1980–81. Geze has followed with its excellent Olymp Junior. Tyrolia has

upgraded to a new 40–80–180 that's excellent, while Salomon has a new and equally fine 127M–137–637 lineup.

* Skis? You name the company, it now has something solid for the kids and juniors—one area where age makes a major difference—although that old Hart Gremlin still holds its own.

* In clothing, everyone at the 1979 show had a big display featuring good, warm, durable outfits, from the skin out. Goggles, hats, mittens, and poles got the same treatment.

In short, March 1979 shall be celebrated as the time when children were emancipated from three decades of ski-manufacturing indifference. March 1980 underscored and expanded the pattern, which kept improving through March 1982.

Still, the (lack of) spirit that gave us those three decades didn't reverse itself in a one-week manufacturers' exposition. Among the good stuff was a heavy residue of antiquated products. Some of the new items were a bit suspect also, especially a few foam-core skis. Some boots were too high and too stiff for most young skiers, pandering to the fashion prejudices of the parents rather than meeting the physical needs of the children. And much of the clothing was just pretty, rather than efficient.

To sum up, the children's market is just like the adults' these days: tricky, competitive, and increasingly expensive. You must do your homework year by year to find the good clothing and equipment, but at least it finally exists. Competition has finally given you a selection among items good and bad, and the suggestions in the following pages should work through 1984, although model names may change. The criteria should hold even longer.

How expensive is it to outfit a child properly for skiing these days? You can't do it for $29.95. Try $299.50. Getting perfectly adequate clothing and equipment that should last for two seasons has to set you back $300 the first year your young skier hits the slopes, maybe a bit less if you pick up a decent pair of skis at a swap. (However, I feel you must get new boots and bindings.) You can save a few dollars by shopping for clothing during March sales, if you're willing to gamble on your child's size next season, but the good bindings rarely come down in price (unless a new model is coming out), and you shouldn't buy boots until the season begins.

But those prices are for children. For juniors—the aggressive, hefty, experienced ten year old and above—forget it. The price of junior racing-quality equipment is roughly $400 itself for boots, skis, and bindings without any allocation for clothing. The bigger kids need bigger sizes and more heft, which tends to cost more (and last a shorter time). Therefore, shop carefully in the spring at the sales.

Remember two key phrases: "Last for two seasons" and "The first year your young skier hits the slopes." With the former, much will depend on how you shop for size (see specifics in the next four chapters). Proper selection of skis, boots, and most inner and outer wear should get you through two years; hats and bindings can last longer; mittens and goggles will last at least two days (until lost); Clothing, especially inner wear, will survive for hand me downs, while other items will double in brass for school and playing in the snow. So $300 isn't an annual expense.

Further, as the latter phrase suggests, you won't have to replace the entire assemblage at list price at the beginning of Year Three. Children's equipment can be recycled quite well, especially if you're dealing on a regular basis with a reputable ski shop. Many will give you a good deal on your child's used skis and boots as trade-ins on new hardware. Some even have formal programs and/or run excellent ski swaps each fall (as do many areas with good kids' programs) where you can find good bargains and will be told honestly when your children can use old bindings for another year or two. Also, if you do enough business with that shop, the owner may even begin to shade the points, or tip you to an equally good (possibly superior) ski, boot, or parka that costs less than your initial choice.

Finding a reputable ski shop can be tough, especially finding one with expertise in children's equipment and clothing. The big discount sport chains tend to be disasters in the junior market; someone in "central buying" finds a manufacturer that will give him his "price points" for specially produced items, usually clothing and skis, and the individual shop managers and salesmen have to sell that merchandise no matter how they feel personally. Most discount shops use standard bindings and boots that sell at standard prices for the top-of-line and as part of cheap packages for the low-end line. Overall, these shops are a no-no. Ditto for department stores and other high-volume merchandisers.

Ski-area shops, especially at the better resorts, consistently carry top-line equipment ("I can't give away the low-priced equipment anymore," said the manager of the Mount Snow shop), but tend to price those items slightly higher than their urban counterparts do (except in resorts like Aspen or Vail, where the sheer number of ski shops keeps the prices competitive and occasionally generates a rash of early sales). However, the main problem with area shops isn't price so much as access; unless you ski at that area regularly, you'll have trouble getting the equipment serviced if it malfunctions. The converse is equally valid—if you regularly ski at one area it may be worth the extra dollars initially to be able to insist on instant service.

Overall, during the past decade, I've concluded that the mid-sized ($250,000–$500,000 annual gross) urban-suburban specialty ski shop—preferably one that's been run for several years by the same husband-wife team—offers the highest probability of your getting quality-price-attention, especially if you live nearby. There are no guarantees: I've seen some wretched shops that follow that profile, but overall I like the odds.

Right behind them are the small, hot-shot, racing-type shops that are run by some aggressive younger man, woman, or couple and are usually located near (but not at) a resort. They'll look to shave a few points on price if you look like you need financial help; but more important, these owners are really turned on by and to good equipment. In New Hampshire (which, like Utah, generally seems to have the best shops in its region), I visited one such shop a couple of years ago where the only junior bindings they carried were Tyrolias. "Anyone wants another binding," the young saleswoman/co-owner said, "I don't want their business." (A bit extreme, perhaps, but it makes the point.) Her choices in skis, from toddler to junior-racer, were quite astute—but as with area shops, generally, access problems to these shops can hurt.

Third in line are small specialty chains, like Carroll Reed (all needs) and KinderSport (mostly clothing), both of which tend to be expensive but adept at selection.

In addition, the family-owned specialty and hot-shot-racing shops tend to develop something of a cracker-barrel aura, and after you've been doing business with them a while, you stop by on off-hours (never on a Saturday before Christmas) and rap about equipment with the owners, the salespeople, and, perhaps best of all, the guy who tunes the skis and mounts the bindings.

Typically, Gail Sweeney—the distaff side of "Norm's," who refers to her regular customers as "my skiers" and "my families," and who mounts photos of the kids she's outfitted on the walls of the shop—lectured me on why fiberfill is better than down, while Norm persuaded me to graduate Greg from a soft 110-cm ski to a stiff 140 because "with those legs he'll outski even a stiff 130 by March." (My fears that 140 would be too long vanished the second day Greg used them.) Then their bindings mechanic touted me off the Tyrolia 50 and onto the 150 for Greg by telling me about that oft hidden (and ignored) boot-binding compatibility problem I'll discuss in Chapter 10. Then, of course, Gail sold us outfits for both kids, and Norm told me to buy Garmonts rather than Nordicas for Alix and to get longer poles for Greg, and the bindings man told me that since *I* had brakes because they were safer than runaway straps, Greg should too, and then we haggled a bit about the trade-ins and . . . well, what the devil, why should I be the only one in the family using top-line everything? Don't my kids have the same rights?

"We have no problems with children. The only problem is with parents."
GAIL SWEENEY
of Norm's Ski Shop, Keene

"Nothing irritates me more than to see the mother who buys herself a $350 skisuit, a $200 pair of boots, and $40 gloves and hats, yet dresses her child in a $16.95 snowsuit she bought at some discount house, and acrylic mittens, and no socks."
JUDY REISS

"Some of the clothing out for children these days is just darling."
SUSAN MCCOY,
fashion editor of SKI magazine

"I've seen a lot of progress these past couple of years. Parents are beginning to learn how to dress their kids for skiing."
BOB KUNKEL

8

HOW DO YOU CLOTHE YOUR CHILD?

This education program on children's ski clothing has been long and hard, and still has a way to go. All of us, we skiing parents, have made a few serious errors along the way, and our kids have paid the price. Greg has a couple of small patches of frostbite, thanks to a goof I made in the winter of 1978–79, because I forgot that kids are far more susceptible to frostbite than adults are (and at far warmer wind-chill factors) and that the best dickeys and goggles aren't worth a damn if they aren't tucked tightly together on cold days. Greg had less than a square inch of surface exposed around each cheekbone that day, and guess what got frostbitten?

This proves that none of us, even we so-called experts, are immune against the goof. Fortunately, I recognized the early-warning signs and minimized the damage to near-zero—but it still shouldn't have happened. You must constantly think about what you're subjecting children to at a ski area, dress them accordingly, and continue to watch the situation.

Few parents know how to dress a child properly for playing in snow and cold weather generally. The challenge is to keep your child warm, dry, and mobile, and the great enemy is bulk. "I've seen some kids so bundled up in thick, heavy clothing that they couldn't move," says Gail Sweeney, "which automatically guarantees they'll get cold. Then the parents come in and ask me for something thicker." No good.

"We try to educate them to the value of proper layering, using *thin* layers of high-quality clothing, because that's the only effective way to keep kids warm," she explains. "We're getting through, finally."

This is probably the one universal article of agreement among the experts. Professionals who'll argue with each other just for the sheer joy of dissent all agree on this point: Layering —a series of intertied, overlapping sets of thin apparel—is everything, provided it is held together by the greatest advance in ski equipment since the step-in binding and the steel edge: the bib overall.

You think I exaggerate? I don't. Any parent who denies his child the protection of the bib overall should be sentenced to a day of skiing at minus 20° with his bellybutton hanging out, because then he'll get a small taste of what his kid feels like dressed in jeans or even fancy racing pants. Bibs aside, kids can disassemble the most intricately and tightly structured overlap any parent can design within seconds of leaving the house to get into the car. Even those ineffective clasps on so-called "racing/ skiing suspenders" merely delay the disintegration until the kid bends over to fasten his safety straps or, if he has brakes, until his first fall or ride on the lift, whichever occurs first. Frankly, to keep a kid warm, a pair of $10 DeeCee overalls may do a better job than a pair of $80 racing pants, but the best bet by far is a pair of bib overalls from one of the better ski-clothing manufacturers (see below).

To complement the bibs, get the matching/contrasting parka. "Kids are hams," Gail says, and as a mother of three and clothier to Keene's hundreds of skiing families she's qualified to comment. "They love colors and looking pretty, and it doesn't cost any more to buy a matching set than to buy the pieces individually."

I'll go even further: It probably costs less. I've tried both routes, and unless you're trying to make do with a cheap parka —an unwise decision in the *long* run—you always seem to spend more piecemeal.

As with all things in this less-than-perfect world, some items in even the best of lines are more equal to the task than others.

If you spend much below $75 for a matching overall-parka suit you're sacrificing something important—the materials and workmanship—and Pam Stenmark of Vail wondered where I shopped that I could find clothing that reasonable! Most of the companies offer high- and low-end models, and you can't tell them apart at a glance. Two separate decisions must be made: one on the insulation, the other on the surface fabric. To weigh this intelligently, you should know what's best and why.

On the insulation, down may be out. Even before the Great Duck Scandal of a few years ago (when the goose feathers developed a high canard content), some of the new synthetic fibers were beginning to render nature's premier insulator obsolete. Polarguard really supplied the coup de goose; it's lighter, better integrated, thinner, dries faster (in both the air and machine), lasts longer, and costs less than down. It's also nonallergenic.

Against this, down's main advantage is that it produces that aggressively nonfashionable look I've always associated with the Boston skier and the backpacking/environmental crowd who'd rather freeze than look pretty. Down is bulky and *looks* warm, and has that "head" advantage of being *natural.* Personally, I've often wondered exactly why plucking the bellies of geese (and ducks and chickens) is better for the ecosystem than making synthetics; but maybe, given the price and availability of petroleum these days, the preservationists have a point.

However, looked at strictly from the vantage point of durability, practicality, and warmth (ignoring fashion completely), the *good* polyesters have the edge. The compacted polyesters, needlepunch and Thermoslim, will hold in body heat, Gail says, and with proper layering underneath will be just as warm as the high-loft polyesters with less layering. For children, most authorities feel, Polarguard is about the best compromise, and, as Gail notes, it has the further advantage of looking and feeling warm to parents. Some of the other inexpensive fiberfills just don't seem to hold up as well on repeated washing-drying cycles, and their initial price advantage often proves, in the long run, to be uneconomical. For those who have heard a rumor that Polarguard was being discontinued, fear not—that has been allayed.

In picking the outer shell, remember that no fabric used in skiwear is waterproof. Nor, frankly, should it be, because a waterproof fabric doesn't breathe. However, several of the nylon-based fabrics are water-resistant (the treatment has to be renewed after several washings) and quite durable—although, as Gail notes, the manufacturers should build reinforced knees into their bib overalls. (You can find some knee patches with waterproof backing and use them for the same effect.) The two most popular nylon fabrics are Antron and Taffeta, with the former costing a bit more because it's softer, drapes better for a more fashionable look, and offers a nicer sheen. (Some cotton-polyester shells aren't as water-resistant but are tougher, Gail says, especially some of the anti-gliss.)

If you opt for anything else, Gail feels, you're being penny-wise and pound-foolish, because the other nylon shells don't hold up well under heavy use or repeated washings and lose their water repellency quickly. If you couple this with a cheap fiberfill, you've got a jacket and bib that, after a few weeks of wear, *might* afford some warmth on a fairly pleasant spring day. "I hate to mention the bad brands by name," she says, "but we had one a few years back where thirty parents returned the bibs within a month. That was some bargain—because many shops wouldn't take them back."

Finally, make sure the cuffs are tight, and long enough or narrow enough to tuck into the mittens with no wrist exposed.

Speaking of brand names, by consensus the best of the children's outfits are produced by Cevas, CG, Roffe, Hot Gear, and Skyr, although you will have to shop the sales hard to get any of them for $75. We've never had much luck with the second line such as Profile or First Team, but my kids beat the hell out of their ski clothing, and "bargains" tend generally to be anything but. Greg was especially fond of his Roffe pullover, which

I have to admit came out of the 1981-82 season in exemplary shape. In ski clothing, by and large, you get only what you pay for.

Tom Montemagni of Mount Snow recommends that no matter which brand you pick, you should lubricate the zippers often with WD-40 to make sure they zip easily.

One final comment here: Avoid those one-piece "snowsuits" or snowmobile outfits; they're cumbersome, bulky, unwieldy, and don't "breathe" well.

Children do not stay warm by parka-and-bib alone. Equally important are good hats, mittens, socks, long johns, turtlenecks, sweaters (or shirts), dickeys, and goggles. Let's take them in my order of importance.

HATS

Wool is better than even the best of the Orlons, provided your child isn't allergic to wool; if he is, obviously, you go with Orlon (although Pam Stenmark suggests sewing a layer of cloth inside the headband "because wool is so much warmer"). With either, however, you must look for a tight weave; those fashionable soft-weave-with-pompom hats are a no-no, especially in the East, Midwest, and northern Rockies, where it does get cold and damp. On the West Coast and through the southern Rockies you can probably survive with a lighter hat, although the humidity on the coast can offset the relatively warmer temperatures for small children. With any hat, look for a double-layer cuff around the ears.

You should be able to get a high-quality hat for $10 to $15, although shops at ski areas and in resort towns may jack that up a bit.

Remember: Children lose much more of their body heat through their heads than adults do. As much as 33 percent of a small child's mass and weight is in his head, against maybe 10 percent for us. I make it a law that both Greg and Alix wear hats even on those lovely spring days when I don't. Whoever said a family unit was a democracy?

MITTENS

Gloves are a firm "NO" for kids below the age of twelve, and even above that age unless they need the superior flexibility of a glove for racing. Mittens are warmer and far more durable, and if you size them properly you can add a thin wool liner for those really cold days when, in fact, you probably shouldn't let them ski in the first place (but, if you're as weak as we are, you will anyway).

The best mittens are made of Polarguard fill and leather covers, but many of us hate to spend $18 to $20 for something kids lose with amazing ease and frequency, no matter how cleverly you think you've got them attached to each other, the parka and/or the child. You can shave maybe $5 with a nylon rather than a leather cover (this is okay), and still another $5 if you opt for a padded foam lining (this isn't). In those cold and damp regions of the East and North, don't drop below the nylon/Polarguard level. Gail Sweeney also dislikes down mittens because they retain water.

Under no conditions should you use those cheap plastic or woven-wool or Orlon ("nets") mittens, unless you like to hear a youngster scream and watch his hands slowly turn blue.

SOCKS

The authorities are beginning to split here, with the majority still favoring the two-sock theory. I agree with the growing minority view that due to the improvements in ski boots for kids (see next chapter), one good pair of thin wool or wool-and-Dacron socks is enough. That's all we use, and with the warmth Greg gets from his Raichles and Alix from her Garmonts, we've had no complaints even on cold days. When, at the end of the season, the boots get a bit tight (from growth of foot and natural expansion in warm weather) and cut off the circulation, producing cold feet, the proper solution is to use a *thinner* sock, not a heavier or second pair.

Tom Montemagni insists that if you use two pairs of socks, put one pair inside the other before you put them on your child; otherwise, putting the second one on pulls the first too tight and cramps the toes.

Don't use tights or leotards, because the fabric is wrong for the feet: It doesn't absorb and dispel dampness, as wool (or even cotton) does. My wife used tights for years and always complained of cold feet (literally as well as figuratively) when mine were quite warm. Three years ago we bought the same model Lange boot (always among the warmest), yet the same pattern existed until Gail Sweeney informed her she'd never be warm with tights. Gail proved to be accurate.

LONG JOHNS

This is a mandatory layer, but it can be formal long johns, jeans, even pajamas (without the foot, however), or union jacks for older children. The one advantage of springing for higher-priced LJs is that the cuffs around the ankles hold up better; cheaper ones, or PJs, get too loose and wrinkle at just the place where you clamp the boots: sheer hell. Jeans are okay because you can pull them up above that juncture, but they get bulky under bibs. Overall, I prefer to spend the extra dollars for good LJs, especially since they can survive well enough to hand down the line—but I have to warn you that at a certain age (about five, alas), little girls don't like to wear little boys' LJs because of the fly. The converse (if yours came in the other order) is more serious pragmatically than emotionally, so perhaps the endurance qualities of good LJs are valuable only if your children are of the same gender.

Incidentally, if you get hung up on this kind of thing, I prefer wearing socks *over* rather than under LJs—at least, until the cuffs on the LJs loosen enough to pull them over the socks. As long as the cuffs stay tight, pull socks over them, which makes it easier to change the socks when (not *if*) they get wet. However, one warning: If the seam where the cuff meets the LJ bottom is too tight, it can cut off circulation in children with thin legs. If so, you have two choices: Either put the LJs over the socks, the easier solution if it works, or use long socks and roll the LJs up to where the seam is above the boot top. At that point, frankly, you'll do just as well with PJs tucked into the socks.

TURTLENECKS

This is another mandatory layer. Cotton is by far the best initially, with its warm-and-dry qualities, but, alas, it shrinks mighty soon in the washing machine. The best compromise is a cotton-and-polyester blend. A good turtleneck can run $10 or more, but again, it endures and can be handed down, and here no gender problems arise (at least, none so far). One thing to watch for is that the neck be long enough to allow at least one fold, preferably two, but that it not be too tight when folded.

SWEATERS AND SHIRTS

This is a key layer. I prefer a good flannel or chamois shirt to a comparable-quality sweater. Good shirts are warm and thin, allowing good mobility; they have pockets inside the zippered parka (invaluable); they can be unbuttoned easily to insert a dickey (or "neck-gaiter"); and priced for quality and warmth, they're cheaper than sweaters (unless you opt for wool rather than cotton, which is unnecessary). Whether you decide on a sweater or a shirt, make sure the garment has a tight weave, is thin and reasonably large, and is machine washable (at the insistence of my wife).

I do prefer a sweater to a shirt under a vest on a warm spring day. True, a lightweight parka is better than a vest, but when your child wants a vest because all the other kids have vests and *you're* wearing one as well, well, you have to bend a little.

DICKEYS (OR NECK-GAITERS)

Although sent by Ullr to protect children from some of our follies, a wool (superior) or Orlon dickey isn't a perfect answer to all problems of wind and cold unless you're attentive. It's among the better forms of protection for a child's face, especially when he's riding a chairlift, and it rolls down as an auxiliary turtleneck. To use it properly, you roll it up to where it overlaps the hat at the ears and covers the tip of the nose, after which you clamp the goggles over the opening to create a (nearly) perfect seal. The problem is that children breathe, which tends to make the dickey wet; if you simply rotate it you can expose another area of skin to the damp material, which then increases the chances of frostbite. What you have to do is continue to reroll the dickey so that the damp places are kept away from the skin, which can be tricky. In any event, a wool dickey is far superior to that hat that pulls down into a face-mask, which guarantees that he'll have a damp spot right in front of nose and mouth around the openings. The best solution, at $20 the pop, is the Scott facemask ($8) attached to Scott goggles ($12).

One important warning: Do not use long scarves. Otherwise responsible people often recommend them, but I equate a scarf with a hangman's noose on most lifts.

GOGGLES AND FACE CREAMS

Goggles are another major protection against the elements—the sunlight and glare as much as the cold. Children's goggles should have green as well as yellow lenses; the former, in fact, may be the more important protection against bright sunlight, because children's eye lenses don't adjust their f-stops as quickly as adults' do. The currently popular orange lenses are a good compromise, but green or gray is best.

Face creams are an even more important protection than goggles. I was rather embarrassed when, reviewing the manuscript for this book, I realized I'd overlooked this item, so I dropped a quick letter off to Dr. Don Overend. His answer tells all you'll ever need to know:

[Many face creams] are very satisfactory, [and the choice] depends on the child's skin type. A blond child who sunburns easily should use a full sunscreen such as "PreSun" liquid or gel (probably the best on the market) or one of the full sunscreen tanning lotions like "Sun Ger," "A-Fil," or the Coppertone full-screen preparation "Sun Bloc." Bonne Bell also makes an excellent full sunscreen under the brand name of "Weather-Proofer." Children whose skins are already partly tanned, or who are olive-skinned and tan a little more easily, could use a lighter weight sunscreen. Most of them, however, particularly young children, have very inactive oil glands and should use some kind of an emollient preparation on the skin to prevent windburn and excessive sun drying, which can cause chapping and discomfort. Fair children should also use a lip protector.

[Children who ski a lot probably don't need a screen once they're well along into the season], but at high altitudes the filter effect of the air on the ultraviolet is much less, so the exposure factor at 11,000 feet is considerably higher than it is at 1,000 feet; plus the reflective effect of the snow, of course, increases the ultraviolet exposure.

Putting it all together so it holds is the final challenge. The best sequence we've found is: undershirt, briefs, turtleneck, long johns/socks, shirt or sweater, bib overalls, parka, hat, goggles, and mittens (have you ever tried to put on a hat or goggles with mittens on?). The dickey is a last-minute optional choice, depending on weather.

Paying for all this, of course, is the initial challenge. I've computed that it costs about $150 to clothe a child for skiing that first year, assuming he doesn't lose too many mittens or hats or leave the goggles home too often. Once you're past that first year, though, you can begin to alternate some of the purchases, and if you play it smart you can alternate the years in which you buy entire new outfits for different kids. At least I keep telling myself it's possible; I just haven't figured out *how* yet.

Further, you can allocate part of the cost to outfitting your child generally for winter. Turtlenecks, shirts, sweaters, and hats are certainly good items to use all winter long, and I've even sent the pair off to school on bad days wearing older bibs-and-parkas. However, let's not fool ourselves: Outfitting a child for skiing isn't cheap, and trying to do it cheaply is the falsest of economies. The last thing you want is an uncomfortable, cold, and miserable child.

"When I think of what the manufacturers used to palm off on kids for ski boots I just get plain furious."
DR. DON OVEREND

"Some of the high, rigid boots being sold now can sure do a hell of a job on a kid's tibia."
DR. MILTON WOLF,
Mount Snow

9

HOW DO YOU
PICK A SKI BOOT?

Picking a pair of boots for a child continues to worry me, even though improvements in the past few years—especially since the first edition of *Kids on Skis* was written—have made the job easier. Now, at last, you can get a pretty good idea if the boot *fits*, but you still have the problem of convincing Junior that he wants the boot you know, with some help from your friends at the ski shop, he should have.

As recently as 1980, you still had to rely mostly on a few sneaky-type tests and a good dose of b'guess and b'gosh. Now, however, *any* boot worth skiing—children's, junior's, and adult's—comes apart, and you can yank out the innerboot and, as with a sneaker, push down and pinch to see how much room there is.

However, you still cannot tell how that foot feels to the youngster when you clamp the buckles—and if he says ouch you have to believe him. Therefore, in the final analysis, if he wants those Screaming Yaller Zonkers, he's going to yell ouch with every other pair and profess comfort in that zonker, whether it's large enough for you or small enough to mold his toes into a hoof.

Boots are unique skiing gear in that they have to serve as both clothing *and* equipment, an important concept. Boots must do two things: provide warmth and comfort, and establish safe control over the skis. When in doubt, however, the former is more important; a little "slop" because the boot is a bit big won't really annoy a young skier until he hits the "E" or "F" levels, and in fact it might even help a beginner, as long as it's not too big. However, nothing will turn a child off skiing faster than cold feet or a blister, because kids aren't quite so adept in the tradeoff department as you and I are. We'll tolerate a little squinch for maximum edge control; they won't.

These days, as part of the price for getting good equipment, children's boots are as complicated to evaluate (and fit) as are adults'. The orthopedists, pediatricians, ski-school people, and shop fitters all disagree widely on how stiff and how high a child's boot should be. I often think I knew more three years ago, before I started interviewing these experts, than I know now. At least I was a lot surer then about the answers: I liked the boot between one-third and halfway up the shin in front, calf height in back, soft to moderate in front–back flex and moderate to stiff in side flex—roughly the same height I use with a slightly softer flex.

Now? I'm not so sure. The boot I liked may be too high and stiff. An interesting episode makes the point. At a *SKI* magazine conference at Copper Mountain in 1978 (see Part IV), Dr. Don Overend commented that, although the evidence was far from conclusive (the evidence was based on "crude experiments with autopsy materials"), he and other experts felt that children have a weak spot one-third of the way up the tibia, and that the boot tongue should run a bit higher than that to disperse and dissipate any breaking force. However, we sent the transcript of the seminar to other experts, and one orthopedist took sharp exception, after which Dr. Overend revised his own opinion to say that "the boot should be at least high enough to protect the tibia and fibular growth zones." Today, most authorities feel we've pushed the boots too high and made them too stiff, and the current theory is to have boots one-third up the front with a slight diagonal rise *up* to the back (see Diagram 1), and a soft flex.

Incidentally, adult boots have followed the same pattern. The butt bumpers of Nordica infamy have all vanished, and as I suggested in the first edition, the "new wave of super-high-

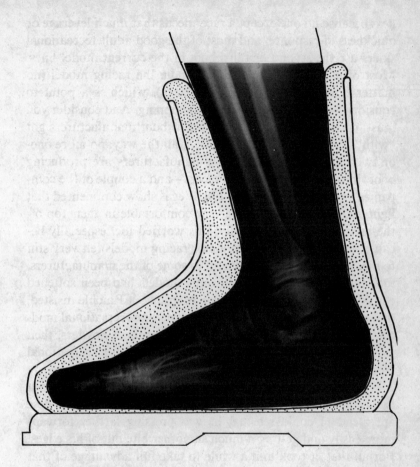

1. *A boot should fit snugly at the heel and ankle, as the diagram suggests, with some room at the toe. The height in back isn't too important, but the height in front should just top the narrow point in the tibia, as the X ray reveals, and not reach too high above that, since it will put too much stress on the knee.*

boots" has failed to catch on. (Good!) At the same time, the "light boot" models of Scott and Garmont have all but totally disappeared. However, almost all of the popular boots have become softer in forward flex, led by the Lange XL-S and its allies, though not necessarily lower and certainly no softer in later flex. Only the true racing models remain stiff in fore–aft flex, because no one except a racer needs that much leverage or quickness of response, and most of the good adult recreational skiers use the second or third boot in the current model lines. Most of us, in fact, can't really handle the racing model (no matter how sexy it looks in the lodge), which is a point to consider when you take your child shopping. And consider you must, carefully. As soon as the major boot manufacturers got "with" the junior market, they went all the way: no more one- or two-model lines. Today the manufacturers are producing boots for toddlers up through racers—and a couple of the companies' representatives at the 1982 Vegas show commented that light adult women would be very comfortable in their top-of-the-line junior boots! Initially, this worried me, especially because, at Vegas, most of the junior racing models felt very stiff to me. Fortunately, they felt stiff to some of the manufacturers, too, and by the following fall some models had been softened considerably—to the degree, Bob Mignone of Raichle insisted, that they skied softer than the top-of-the-line recreational models. He suggested that I have Greg ski a pair of Spyders, then the top junior racer in their lineup, against the top recreational Nordica he was using.

No contest. Greg got into those Spyders and needed about two runs—or was it two *turns?*—before he proclaimed, "These are great!" I could see that he was pressing farther forward more easily and getting a much smoother bite out of his edges. For all that, it took him a while to take full advantage of that superior boot (the better part of the season, in fact), but there was no question that he improved technically a lot faster than he had been doing with the Nordicas—which I could never get him back into!

But remember that Greg is a big, husky kid with lower legs like fireplugs; against that, if he finds a junior racer easier to flex, won't everyone? More important, Greg is an aggressive, competent, and experienced skier, which means he's more apt to be able to get the full measure out of a better boot. If I had to offer a conclusion based on performance, I'd recommend that any youngster eighty pounds or better who skis relatively well and often should use the junior racer.

But, you counter, what about the cost? Aren't they twice as expensive, give or take a few bucks? Positively. A junior racer will run anywhere from $100 to $175, with a strike point in the $140 range, while a good top-recreational boot can run as little as $50 to $60. Those are the facts. The decision is strictly personal and subjective: Does he need the better boot, and will he get enough mileage out of it to earn back the dollars? I guess the answer is simply this: What would you do for yourself?

Compounding the problem is that a junior racer has to fit more closely than a top-recreational model, for the same reasons that a top-of-the-line adult model has to: with performance equipment, slight errors are magnified. What this really means, of course, is that *you* have to learn how to retrofit boots to give your child both top performance and two seasons' use. It's not hard to learn—I've gotten pretty good at it, actually—but it does have to be learned.

In any event, I hope this makes one crucial point, which I tried to emphasize in the introduction to this edition: Today, we have a children's market and a juniors' market. Recreational models, as I see them, are designed for children, whereas racing models are keyed for juniors. This distinction is based only partly on age and size; equally, maybe more important are the commitment and competence and the personality and the frequency, yours as well as your child's.

Another tricky decision concerns materials: Which are best for inner boot and shell? The best shells, adult and junior, are still made of polyurethane, which has the durability of tempered steel, resists scuffs and slashes, doesn't wear down at toe and heel easily, and has a consistent forward flex. For this, however, you pay heavily. The less-durable thermoplastics (whatever their trade name) cost less and last less.

Those who are pro poly-u argue that kids scuff their boots more, walk in them more, wear down the heels and toes far more (producing potentially serious problems for binding adjustments), and slash the sides more with their ski edges. One ski-school director commented rather drily that "an aggressive kid will put five seasons' worth of wear on a boot in a tough week."

Those who are anti poly-u state that, at best, kids will get two seasons' wear out of a pair of boots, or forty to fifty days at the most, unless you live at a ski area. A good poly-u shell (like Lange's) will last *me*—and I ski hard—at least 150 to 200 days, and still be in skiable shape. Why pay for all that unused durability for kids' boots? In addition, most of the thermoplastics flex more softly (except on frigid days), weigh less, and provide more than adequate edge control.

The solution? Simple. Get poly-u, and damn the cost. Why? Because two years ago the approved safety standards under the American Society of Testing and Materials (ASTM) system said that only poly-u works well with bindings, whether junior or adult. There's enough room in the testing methodology to allow *some* of the non poly-u boot soles to qualify, but most of the bindings manufacturers insist on poly-u or "all bets are off." Really, what counterargument exists to that?

On liners, I prefer cloth to leather because cloth dries more quickly, and the last thing I feel like doing at the end of a ski day is to remove the liners from the shells to dry. However, Gail Sweeney insists I should do that even with the cloth liners to make sure my children's feet stay dry. Now, even if they haven't complained about cold and wetness, I compromise to the extent that I remove the boots from the knapsacks and expose them to the heat vents at home. In any event, avoid those furry-type liners that look warm, because they hold water, compress quickly, and begin to shed like a hound dog in spring.

As I mentioned in the introduction to this edition, several companies are now making junior boots and a few are making good kids' boots. My selections there are based on my best research, at the 1982 Las Vegas show and on the mountains with Greg and Alix—and almost all of them are pretty decent. Your major decision should focus on how well they fit.

As we all know, children's feet don't always grow in the most predictable progressions. Sure, a ski-shop owner will tell you that properly fitted boots *should* last for two seasons. But that owner is keeping his fingers crossed just as we are, because he knows as well as I do that come late in December that second season, Gregory is apt to look at me painfully on a chairlift and tell me his feet are cold "and the shell is pinching my little toe." His prior pair lasted two seasons and Alix's have lasted two, but this pair of Nordicas didn't. Accepting the inevitable, I went back to Norm's, found the right size for two seasons' use in a pair of the previous season's leftovers (but new), a model higher in the line; I haggled and traded a bit, and presto, Greg had a new pair of boots for the balance of the season and, hopefully, all of the next. (Actually, they would have lasted even longer, but early in that following season we shifted to the Spyders.)

Even allowing for normal growth, fitting a pair of boots to get two seasons' use is tricky. If the boot is too large, the foot will slip inside the liner and shell and blister the heel, bang the front of the instep, and afford very little control. Also, a child should *never* use more than two pairs of socks while skiing (Greg, like me, uses only one), and the inner sock shouldn't be so thick that his feet perspire, and quickly get cold. However, a child's big toe shouldn't be as close to the boot end as an adult's.

To make fitting easier, a couple of the manufacturers have removable inner soles inside the removable inner liners, which provide the best way to judge the fit: Remove the inner sole, then put it against your child's foot. If he's got about an inch of extra length he *should* get two seasons' wear from the boot.

If the boot you and the shop like doesn't have a removable inner sole, the old two-finger test is still as good as any: Without buckling the boot (which I think is obvious, but experts tell me to mention it), slip your middle and index fingers between the child's heel and the back of the inner liner; if both fingers fit

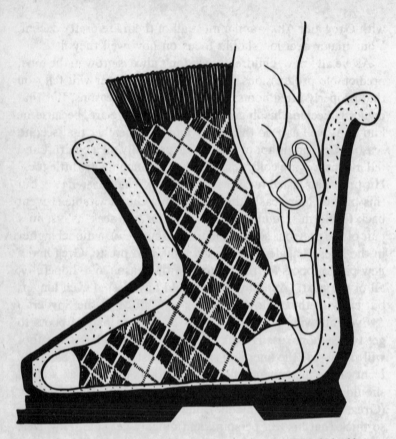

2.   *When all else fails, the old, reliable two-finger test will work. With the buckles open,
insert your hand as indicated above. This compresses both the liner and the child's heel
much the same as the closed boot will, and the two fingers will approximate an inch of
clearance at the toe when the boot is buckled.*

snugly you've got that same inch (allowing for compression of
both the material and your child's heel). The index finger
alone will give you one season, or the proper fit for a racing
boot (see Diagram 2). However, as I said earlier, I can't imagine anyone these days opting for a boot that doesn't have a
removable inner sole.

When you buckle the boot, the heel will be pushed back into the pocket and adequate space be created for the toes. Test the former by holding down the shell and asking your child to raise his heel; one-quarter inch is fine.

Kids need even more free space in which to wiggle their toes than adults do. The area from the ball of the foot forward should be quite loose. Alas, it's very hard for you (or the shop fitter) to test that; even removing the liner won't really tell you much, because the shell will compress space, material, and toes.

I've come up with one ad hoc test, though, that may work. If the length seems right after the two-finger test but Junior can lift his heel more than one-quarter inch inside the boot, you probably have the extra space around the toes. Then, to solve the lift problem, use some of those heel-fitting/tightening kits available for adults' boots (with which you should be quite familiar). Become adept with those pads, duct tape, and scissors —I carry the mess with me—and as your child's foot grows you can trim them, then remove them totally. Equally good are those Nordica plastic heel cups I've taken to using. Ask for them *free* at any shop.

Some ski shops may disagree with all, much, or some of this advice, but no one has ever said that boot fitting is a precise science. In April 1980, after a day of skiing at Stratton, we stopped at a highly respected ski shop in Bondville, where I had Greg try on several pairs of boots. The fitter—quite knowledgeable about equipment, let me add—was aghast at the size Norm had given Greg in January. "Much too large," he said, and proceeded to fit Greg so perfectly in a pair of Langes that, had it been November and had I bought them, I'd have been fortunate to get into February before having to buy another pair. And how "too large" were those Nordicas? Greg had managed to find enough control in them to win a NASTAR gold in February and had had no trouble earlier that day in April keeping up with me through those big, soft moguls of spring! Translation: I agree with Norm's theory.

Also not a science is any buckling system on kids' boots.

Garmont's seem to have an edge on Nordica's, because at four and a half Alix could more or less buckle her boots while Greg, at eight, never could master his. At nine, with his new pair, he succeeded. Generally, soft, long bales (the loops) seem incompatible with metal notched levers in a child's hands, but I guess it's good to know parents are useful for something besides transportation and food.

The only buckling system that children have no trouble handling is Lange's, which I've long regarded as the best on the adult market. At the age of four, Alix had less trouble buckling and unbuckling my big Langes than she did with her own Garmont's, but the problem is that, aside from the buckles, Lange has never produced a good boot for children. The old orange junior Banshee (the XL-100), their one long-time entry into this market, has traditionally been a stiff junior racer; it may well have been discontinued by the time you read this, but many pairs will linger in the shops. A new junior model, based on their rental unit, is now available, but I just haven't had a chance to run it through any tests. I hope it finally produces a "viable option," because Lange has always been my favorite adult boot, and even the Raichle Flexon-5 hasn't moved me out of the XL-S. But Lange has remained uncommitted to the children's market and less than overpowering even in the junior market.

Dynafit had done something interesting: It designed a toddler boot with a single-buckle rear-entry system, with the "tongue" working as a shoehorn. It came up with this design, I'm told (I'll believe it because it makes a good yarn) by tossing several prototypes of this and different models into a nursery and asking the kids to pick the one they could enter and buckle most easily. Truth is, little kids do hunker a lot better than we can and seem to get good leverage in that position. In contrast, I threw a pair of K2 boots with a comparable system the length of the Stowe base lodge one morning after fifteen minutes of failure, cursing and sweating, while two friends laughed themselves sick. So perhaps the problem is that kids are different and can't quite work with an adult buckling system.

However, even though this buckling system offered some help, the boot itself didn't: As with many rear-entry boots (like the Hanson and, for my money, the Salomon), the front of the boot, with nothing to break its mass, proved too stiff for youngsters (and adults) to flex softly and easily. So it was discontinued.

"Sometimes I think the good Lord knew we'd never make a binding to fit a child, so he made children to fit bindings. It's the only explanation I have as to why more kids aren't smashed up every season."
NORM SWEENEY

10

HOW DO YOU PICK A BINDING?

There is a lot of truth in the facing quotation, because youngsters fall funny. Funny as in strange, in weird positions, rather than funny as in ha-ha (although that, too, on occasion). At one conference a couple of years ago at Mount Snow, Dr. Milton Wolf—who's probably treated as many injuries as anyone in skiing—commented about both the positions and the survival mechanisms: "I saw one child last year whose leg had caught in a pile of snow and his foot was pointed roughly a hundred eighty degrees different from his knee. 'Oh Jeez,' I thought as I heard him screaming, but as I gently pulled his leg loose it just flipped around, *whoong,* and the kid laughed, got up, and skied off. An adult in that position would have been in traction for a month or more."

I agree. During the early years I've extricated Greg from entangled-spill positions no adult could ever get into, much less survive, and Alix has this one forward/reverse-wedge flop that defies description. If I seem to dwell on this overmuch it's because I must make one basic point: Adult falls are far more predictable as far as position and torque (twisting force) are concerned, and adult-binding designers have spent decades studying and compensating for these positions and torque factors. For all that, fully half (if these statistics are accurate) of adult injuries could not have been prevented by designing a better binding because the injuries aren't caused by bindings at all; the falls produce no torque at the foot, which is what is attached to the ski.

So where does this leave us with children, whose positions

and torque are even less predictable than adults'? Your first reaction could be one of frustration and futility: Why bother? If half of adult injuries can't be prevented, what's the proportion among kids?

But I prefer to read those figures another way, because hidden among the gloom is a high note of optimism: We've reached that 50 percent of unpreventable injuries range only because the number (and proportion) of preventable injuries has been significantly reduced by better bindings (and boots) these past few years. The competitive bindings marketplace has forced manufacturers to produce better adult bindings and, within the past three years, better children's bindings as well.

What a change it's been in so short a time. In 1976–77, when Greg got his first "real" skis and bindings, my choice was between the Look GTK and the Salomon 101—and I must admit that *I* wouldn't have skied on either damned one of them. On the traditional "1–10 scale," I rated Salomon about 1 and Look about 1.3. I didn't begin to relax about Greg's bindings until two years later, when I finally put him into a pair of Tyrolia 150s. (For those who know that's an adult binding, I'll explain the decision later.) Tyrolia has since refined that 50 – 150 line into the excellent 30 –60 –160 series, while Salomon finally began producing an adequate number of its equally good two-model 127 system. To round out the current trio of superior children's step-in bindings, Geze introduced its Olymp Junior model in the spring of 1980—*possibly* the best of them all and certainly the most expensive. At the same time, Burt designed the children's version of the adult Burt II and, for my money, blew Besser into antiquity in the plate-binding area. (Burt gets annoyed when I call his binding a plate, but it *is.*)

Now, I'm not a bindings expert, but I have spent a lot of time with people who are: the mechanical engineers who design them, pediatricians and orthopedists who ski a lot and treat injuries, ski-school and nursery supervisors who live with the results, and the marketing people who have to defend and explain their designers' decisions against those produced by other companies. So over the past seven years, I've developed a strong "journalistic feel" about what works—pragmatically, functionally, even esthetically. Let's get very basic.

A binding has to do only two things: (1) attach the ski to the boot as firmly as possible, to allow the maximum amount of edge control as the knee-ankle lever transmits movement orders to the ski (this function is called *retention*); and (2) eject the ski from the boot, to dissipate the torque that otherwise would do unpleasant things to that knee-ankle lever, such as break or severely sprain it. The second function is known as *release,* and every binding except the Burt does this by literally removing the ski from the boot when a certain degree of twist is developed. Burt prefers to use a pair of long cables to dissipate the force sufficiently without actually ejecting the skis, then bring them back in contact with the boots. However, the difference between the Burt and the others isn't infinite. All good bindings have some degree of elasticity—which means the unit will release the boot partially to dissipate the torque, then return the boot to "center"—unless the torque is sufficient to pass the point of no return and blow the boot out of the binding. (As you might suspect, bindings designers and marketers disagree loudly about how to create and measure that elasticity and how much of what kind of twist is needed—and they can all be very convincing.)

Let's get even more basic. A step-in release binding has three separate parts: the toe, the heel, and the brake. Each does different things, and while all major designers create well-integrated systems, some designs are better than others. (The salespeople also make a big promotion out of their anti-friction devices [AFDs], usually Teflon skid pads; but since all good bindings now have them, why bother discussing them? Just keep them clean.)

TOEPIECES

Two different types finally exist for children as they long have for adults: the pincer and the single-pivot. In the former, only the wings move—more precisely, only the one wing being pressured (see diagram 3). In the latter, either the entire toepiece or the entire toe-lockdown pivots around a central post. The pincer is logically the better concept: Less mass has to move, the opposite "wing" can't bind up the boot, and (I'll get some argument here) the spring settings can be adjusted more precisely to allow for better elasticity.

The basic pincer toe is the Marker, which Geze uses under a patent license but somehow seems to use better, at least in the children's unit. The wings on the child's Marker M-5 haven't quite as good a return-to-center mechanism as the adult models, while the wings on the Geze Olymp Junior are as well engineered as on the top-of-the-line adult Olymp 950. Tyrolia has developed its own version of the pincer, but the functional difference is insignificant. Rate Geze and Tyrolia excellent.

The single pivot is ubiquitous, although Look is the only company never to have lost faith in it. Salomon used a single pivot before shifting to a double pivot in the 505 and 555 adult models (though even then it stayed with that single pivot, albeit not brilliantly, in its junior 101/111 series). Geze and Marker began with single pivots before shifting to pincers, and Geze still uses a single pivot at the low end of its adult line. Salomon has now returned to the single pivot—a highly sophisticated version—throughout its 737, 637, 137, and 127 lines, and they're really very good.

"None of those old single-pivot models worked well for kids," Norm Sweeney says, "especially those that depended on a ball-bearing resting in a cup. Under some twisting conditions, the release setting on a ball-bearing system could increase twenty-fold," he says, "and constant use simply wore out the release mechanism. It was just no good, but for far too long it was all we had." Fortunately, the new Salomon 137 mirrors the sophistication of the 737 and 637 and avoids those problems. Look's children's models are equally good.

HEELPIECES

If you like a touch of irony, it was with the heel unit that Tyrolia leapfrogged over the competition a few years ago: the diagonal release in the top-of-the-line adult 350 (now 280 and

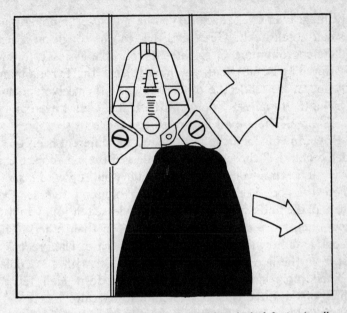

3. *In the pincer toe above (based on the Geze Model), only the left wing (small arrow) moves to allow the boot to eject to the left (large arrow); the rest of the binding remains stationary. In the single-pivot (not shown), the top of the binding swings to the right at the same time—a more massive movement.*

380) models, and the *only* release a child could manage himself in the 50-150 (now 40-80-180) series. But only a few years later, Geze and Salomon may have leaped over Tyrolia in that same children's-heel sector by developing units that are easier to enter (but not to release).

In theory, a heel works simply: You step in and you step out. However, since the heel must lock in your boot when you're skiing, you obviously have to release *something* manually before you can step out voluntarily, and in the *old* Look (I can tell you firsthand, having spent two seasons as Greg's auxiliary heel releaser) "voluntarily" was a sometime thing, as in, "sometimes even I couldn't do it without effort." In the Tyrolia and Geze, you have to *lift* a lever to release; in the Salomon you have to *depress* it. After using all three myself (adult and junior models are similar here), I'll give Tyrolia and Salomon a slight advantage over Geze, because you have to insert a pole tip into a small notch in the Geze, and that can be tough on a small child's coordination. Greg rates Tyrolia the easiest. *However,* lest anything be clear-cut, you have to cock the Tyrolia manually to get in, while the other two cock themselves, making Tyrolia the toughest. You want the truth? Call it even among those three: They're all first-rate.

How can you confirm this? Just test the different heels on the "demo boards," those working models in the ski shop. Clamp them all down into locked position, then pull upward *inside*— where the boot heel will be on an involuntary release. Even when all the units are set for the same release tension, you'll see how much more easily some "blow" open than others. Then recock it and try the outside voluntary release. Then recock it, put it on the floor, stand on it, and work it with a ski pole.

Then, more important, have your child do it. He'll tell you which of the three is easiest for him to operate.

Look's position in the "heel market" is hard to define in a few quick words, so I'll take more. At the top of the market, the new 99 (light) model with its refined rotamat is as good as the Tyrolia 280D, the Geze 950, and the Salomon 637, with which it competes for the *junior* skier (see that discussion in the boot chapter). Greg rates it flat even with the Tyrolia, previously his favorite, and ahead of the others. But I've never been quite as satisfied with their *children's* models, which have fixed rather than rotating heels. I just feel that their competitors make more substantially built step-in models, which is what everything from the 07 through the 57 really is, but nobody makes a better rotamat, including Marker.

BRAKES

If anything, a brake is more important for a child than for an adult, because in addition to the obvious safety advantage— eliminating the pinwheeling ski—kids can have the dickens of a time fastening a safety strap (talk about the ultimate misnomer). Also, good brakes offer an easy way to lock the skis together for carrying, which I sometimes think is their ultimate advantage from my viewpoint.

However, to work well a brake should be integrated into the heel design. No matter what the designers say, brakes that work under the toe or sole *can* apply upward force at the wrong place at the wrong time and restrain the toe on release. This is my only real quarrel with Look, which places its brakes under the boot sole. However, Greg had no problem with it, so perhaps —as Look's Jean-François Lanvers told me—my objection is more philosophical than real. Finally, those add-on brake units, by very definition, produce an independent force that may compete with, rather than complement, the binding's design. Geze, Salomon, and Tyrolia all have fine integrated brake units under the heel, although the Geze can be tricky to lock together for carrying. Sometimes it defeats me.

The plate binding is totally different from the heel–toe step-in, American in concept and design where the step-in is Austrian (Tyrolia), French (Salomon and Look), and German (Geze and Marker); the conceptual differences are as wide as the ocean between them. Essentially, the plate binding dismisses any concern for the condition of the boot sole (and doesn't worry overmuch about the shape or size either), because all retention-release functions are controlled by the two pieces of the binding, the mounting and the plate. The plate is attached (permanently in some Spademans) to the boot and doesn't release from the boot in a fall; instead, it releases from the second part of the binding, which is mounted to the ski. Release in a fall is every bit as total as in a step-in (except for the Burt, whose cables dissipate the torque, then pop the plate back on). Thus, all aspects of release-retention are controlled within the binding and provide (theoretically) perfect metal-to-metal or plastic-to-plastic contact, and because of the design provide infinite angles of release at heel and toe above the plane of the ski and snow.

However, plate bindings still have two weaknesses: a tendency (because of the mass and proximity of the plate and/or mounting) to interrupt and change the designed flex pattern of the ski, and an even more pronounced tendency to prerelease (eject you from the ski when it shouldn't) at designed settings (least pronounced in the Burt). In addition, many plate bindings are difficult to get back into when you've ejected on the hill —little problem with the Besser, but more with the Burt if the cables hang up in soft snow.

Another consideration is weight—the child's, not the binding's. Until Tyrolia introduced its 30 model for the 1979–80 season, you couldn't find a step-in unit that was safe below a child's weight of thirty-five pounds, and even that was the absolute minimum—meaning, frankly, that no child weighing less than forty pounds should have used one, no matter what the literature says or how much of a safety factor is built in.

The Tyrolia 40 has a minimum safe weight of twenty-two pounds. Allocating a 10 percent safety factor (as I do), any child weighing twenty-five pounds can have all the advantages of the Tyrolia 80 (fifty-five-pound rated minimum) in a smaller, equally well-executed and well-designed binding. That was the lowest release-weight of any step-in binding currently on the market by nearly ten pounds—an amazing further jump on the competition—until Geze equaled it for 1980–81 with the Olymp Junior and Salomon topped them all with "*no* minimum weight." Since no one below twenty-five pounds needs a real binding anyway, rate them all even in this department.

Before that, the Besser Child's model (not the Junior) dropped down safely to thirty pounds—if you could find one. I did, but the binding, while simple and efficient, kept working loose of its setting, and poor Alix kept prereleasing. While I might have used a lock-tight solution on a good metal binding, that plastic frightened me.

A new question has arisen of late: Is weight the crucial test? Most bindings are rated on this basis (mainly because that's how parents think about their children: Is the binding safe at forty-three pounds?). However, Marker prefers to rate its setting based on the thickness of the tibia, the key bone in the lower leg, because that's where the major breaking force in a fall is often applied. (For instance, a strong, aggressive skier can weigh two hundred pounds, but if the binding is set for that weight and he has a thin tibia the binding could be set too high and crack his leg.) Geze also added a tibia chart for 1980–81.

The industry is still wrestling (quietly) with this question, but some of the better ski shops have long measured the tibia as a secondary check of the binding setting. Thus, you might want to get hold of a Marker booklet and see how its settings compare on a tibia basis with the weight-based settings of any other binding you may buy. Since virtually all bindings companies have shifted from their individual setting scales to a universal, or DIN, scale, you should be able to persuade your ski shop to find the best and safest setting based on both weight and tibia thickness.

Weight and size produce still another decision/problem: Compatibility—should you choose a child's binding because your child's age says he's a child? Should you shift to an adult binding as soon as your child reaches that unit's minimum weight (adding that 10 percent safety factor)? Or must you consider another criterion, boot-sole size? This problem is less serious if you select plate bindings. You don't have to worry about the shape of or wear-and-tear on the toes and heels of the boot because the plate bindings' release is strictly internal and they're easier to adjust for size if more than one child uses the pair of skis. (Great for hand-me-downs.) And among the plate bindings, the Burt is so far ahead of the competition that, for my money, I would no longer even consider any of the other, more traditional plates. For *your* money, you have to make your own decisions, but as with the step-ins, make sure your child can work the unit, including getting back into it after a fall-ejection, before you buy any other plate.

*"I'd like to see how well you'd do on that mountain with a
pair of plastic skis without edges."*
NANCY ALFARO,
when I brought Alix, at four and a half,
into the Mount Snow nursery for a lesson

11

HOW DO YOU PICK A PAIR OF SKIS?

Mea culpa. I guess I just wasn't ready to release my little girl totally at four and a half, so after I bought her those excellent Garmont boots and adequate Besser bindings, I had to maintain something of the baby. So I mounted the bindings on a pair of edgeless, solid plastic Yaller Dragons we had kept from Greg's early days, and it was a mistake!

As soon as kids are ready for lessons, they're ready for real skis.

Still, I was right on one level: Of all the necessary equipment, skis rank last. Good clothing and boots are a must for comfort and control, and proper bindings are mandatory for safety. But until a youngster reaches the "E" and "F" levels in ski school, almost any ski with an inset edge, decent construction, and proper length will do.

As always, *almost* is the key word, because every so often a ski comes onto the market that's a real dog. Even the big companies come a cropper on occasion. Rossignol, which made up one of the best junior skis ever crafted—the old (and, sadly, discontinued) Strato 105 Junior that Greg loved so dearly—created a disaster in the children's group a few years ago: the Smash J. This was an error in design, because the rods running the length of the foam core could blow out the sidewall if you mounted the bindings improperly (and sometimes even if you did this correctly). Fortunately, Rossi caught the problem quickly and superseded the Smash J with the Jaguar, which Alix used without problem for two seasons (and which I'm passing down to my nephew to see if it will last another two), even though it feels like it's a relatively flimsy ski compared, say, to a Fischer Target or some of the heftier foam-core Austrian skis. So be careful: A child should get two good years out of a pair of skis, and you want to buy a ski you can mount and forget, not have to return for repairs or replacement.

The first requirement is that inset edge, just like on adult skis. Forget, ignore, eliminate forever from your consideration those cheap wood skis with the edges screwed on; they don't work. The edge has to be integral to and flat with the bottom of the ski. A child's ski has to be just as flat, smooth, and slick as yours (it doesn't hurt if you sharpen the edges occasionally, either), and those screw-on jobs cannot be tuned. I'll admit that you don't have to keep the skis of a five-year-old beginner quite as well tuned as yours (should be), but by the time he reaches that "E" or "F" level you may have to tune them more often than yours because hard-skiing juniors chop up the bottoms something fierce. But whether four or twelve, when a youngster is ready to take lessons, even at the nursery level, he needs that inset edge.

Construction—how the ski is built and what it's built from (wood, foam, metal honeycomb, and so on)—has become an increasingly controversial issue over the past few years. For all the improvements in foam-injection techniques and materials, the wood-core ski remains more durable and consistent. It also costs a lot more, and unless your child is a solid intermediate who logs twenty or more days in a season, you won't get your money's worth. But if your youngster is good and skis a lot . . . well, Alix's improvement by shifting from a foam Jaguar to a wood Target was a lot more dramatic than just the extra length alone could possibly have provided, and even length for length, you could see a notable difference.

Foam has an inherent advantage over wood: The density of the foam injected into the core can be decreased as the ski's length decreases, producing the same flex throughout the model's size range. This is much harder for a manufacturer of a wood-core to do, with the result that the smaller sizes in a model tend to get much stiffer (to the point where some have all the flexibility of a two-by-four). Thus, for small children the foam-core is usually preferable.

But not always. Alix got her Jaguars back in 1979–80 because she couldn't flatten (see page 117) any of the wood-cores, but two years later, at fifty-five pounds, she had no similar problem with the Target at 120cm, that ski's shortest length.

For juniors like Greg, big and strong and aggressive, wood is the only answer. Some foam-core skis, even those made by good companies, can break down under the battering they get from hard-skiing juniors.

While you're looking at construction, make sure the shovels (front ends) flex softly so that your child won't bury his tips in soft snow or get bounced around too severely in the bumps. The overall flex can be a bit stiffer, especially if you ski a lot in the East or Midwest.

Length, of course, is important, but here, alas, no firm mathematical formulas apply in deciding how long the ski should be. I still worry about it in alternating years for each child, because (1) I want to get two years' use for each child on each pair of skis; and (2) I don't want the ski to be too long early in the first season or too short late in the second (good luck).

Between these last two perils, the first is more important; a child has to be able to handle those skis the second day he's on them or he'll dislike them forever. If they're a bit short by the second spring, it's no major tragedy. After all, I often drop down to a short ski when the snow gets wet and heavy in the spring.

You'll hear a lot of ad-hoc rules on ski length offered even by the best ski shops—chest height for beginners, chin height for better skiers, etc.—but this fails to cover one major difference among children: weight versus height. Greg is a big, robust boy, while Alix is a bit light for her height; therefore, how can a chest–chin–scalp rule apply correctly to both? It can't, unless your child is absolutely average. Rossignol now prints the recommended weight on its children's skis, but others still don't. What do you do then?

What I've found most effective is the card-and-camber test, or, to put it another way, try *my* ad-hoc test rather than a ski shop's. I place a card beneath the middle of the ski (right below the boot's sole), then ask the child to stand on the ski. If I can remove the card with a gentle but solid tug, the ski's the right length, as happened with Alix and a 100cm Jaguar. If it slips right out it's too long, as occurred with Alix and a 100cm Fritzmeier. If you can't pull it out except by using real force, it's too short. You should be able to find a happy tug; if not, try another model or brand.

Why does this test work? A few basics:

* To work effectively, a ski must be flat on the snow (see diagram).

* A child cannot counterflex a ski unless he's big and aggressive as well as experienced and competent, and even then it's questionable.

A ski is a delicately balanced, high-performance machine (at those prices it better be). Different skis are designed to do different things well—float in powder, cruise on hardpack, cut on ice—and each type of ski has its own characteristics. Powder or low-speed cruising skis tend to be softer in flex with a corresponding higher camber (arch in the middle of the ski), while ice and high-speed cruising skis tend to be stiffer with a correspondingly lower camber. In addition, skis designed to handle well in bumps and softer snow have a soft, highly flexible shovel, while racing skis tend to be stiffer from tip to tail. These days, thanks to the new materials that either replace or augment the wood core, you can find some high-performance adult skis that can do all those things reasonably well. But that degree of technology hasn't really invaded the child's market yet, except maybe for junior racer skis. You have to go one way or the other, and until a child is firmly into racing you should opt for

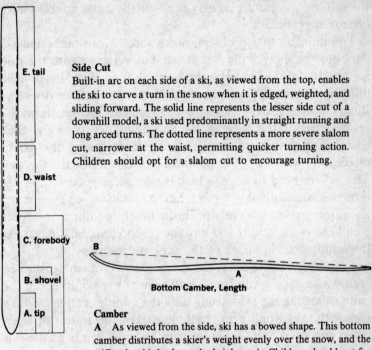

E. tail

D. waist

C. forebody

B. shovel

A. tip

Side Cut

Built-in arc on each side of a ski, as viewed from the top, enables the ski to carve a turn in the snow when it is edged, weighted, and sliding forward. The solid line represents the lesser side cut of a downhill model, a ski used predominantly in straight running and long arced turns. The dotted line represents a more severe slalom cut, narrower at the waist, permitting quicker turning action. Children should opt for a slalom cut to encourage turning.

Bottom Camber, Length

Camber

A As viewed from the side, ski has a bowed shape. This bottom camber distributes a skier's weight evenly over the snow, and the stiffer the ski the *lower* the height at **A.** Children should opt for a softer ski with a higher arch at **A.**

B The dotted line represents the most common way of determining length, but some companies mark it as if the ski were totally flat instead of having a turned-up tip.

Flex Curve

Flex

Variation in stiffness or bending properties throughout the length of a ski; thicker and stiffer at the midsection, thinner and more flexible tip and tail. The solid line illustrates a ski with an even flex curve. The dotted line depicts the uneven flex curve of a ski with a stiff tail relative to its forebody, which is useful for children who otherwise might bury ski tips in soft bumps.

the softer ski, meaning he may occasionally have trouble on ice or frozen granular.

To minimize that problem, make sure he can push that ski flat onto the snow. This is somewhat at variance with the rule for good adult skiers, who tend to use long skis for ice. The difference is important, because a strong adult skier does one thing children usually cannot do: He puts all his weight on the inside edge of the turning ski and angulates strongly, thus eliminating that extra camber and counterflexing the ski in direct ratio with the arc of his turn. (At least that's the theory.) This is very hard to learn, which is why some good advanced– intermediate adult skiers often have trouble on ice even when using the proper equipment. This is much too much to expect a child to learn, and if you buy the ski too long he'll never get the middle, cutting edge of the ski onto the ice.

Conversely, if the ski is too short, the weight isn't dispersed evenly along the entire length and edge of the ski; in effect, the child is bowing the ski—using only the middle section—which means the ski won't grip anything except the softest of snow and won't track well—that is, grip the snow firmly as the skis run straight ahead, which children so dearly love to do.

The only advantage of putting a small, light, beginning skier on a short board is that with so little of the ski on the snow, the child can turn (swivel) it more easily: the old Graduated Length Method concept. That's all right for those initial lessons, I guess, but it definitely means you won't get two seasons out of that ski. Besides, GLM hasn't worked that well with children, and I've learned (first- and secondhand) that kids adapt rather well and quickly to the proper length ski, especially if you give them no other option.

Thus the card test described above: Too much tug tells you the child will bow the ski in the middle on a straight run, too little shows he won't get the middle down. Obviously, if you can't find perfection or if your child has been growing rapidly, get the *slightly* longer ski. But in no event, until he's racing, should the length be much above the top of his head (to use that ski-shop ad-hoc test and eat a few of my own words).

Any other problems? An aggressive youngster will chop the guts out of the tops of his beautiful new skis, so live with it. The tops of Greg's skis after three days looked like mine after thirty. If possible, try to find a ski with a reinforced metal top edge (as more and more are beginning to include), but don't put too high a priority on it. Some parents apply a thin coat of hard clear lacquer to the top, then fill in the new cuts to prevent water (melting snow) from seeping in and swelling the wood core— a good idea. But children's skis do not stay pretty for long. Children's egos, unlike yours, are involved with using their skis, not in how nice they look.

For juniors ready for racing-quality skis, you have one more choice to make: SL (slalom) versus GS (giant slalom) models. I lean strongly toward GS models because they demand a more precise technique to master, but kids will opt for the SL because it's quicker. The GS tends to be smoother and faster in a schuss, more stable for (sigh!) getting air, and generally better in soft snow, while the SL handles better in bumps (if it has a soft tip) and is often more precise on ice.

I suppose, in conclusion, I have to name some of the better skis now on the market, so with fingers and toes crossed here goes.

For juniors, the Austrians seem to have the edge, especially the wood-core models made by Head, Fischer, and Atomic. For those who prefer the pizzazz of the French, I prefer Dynastar to Rossi because its foam-cores seem more durable.

For children, many companies make an acceptable "squirt ski" (foam-core): all of the above plus Kastle, Blizzard, Kneissl, and the perennial Hart Gremlin (now foam, but still stiff). Overall, the model names change faster than the structure and design, so don't get too hung up on cosmetics.

"My poles are like the controls of a helicopter."
GREGORY BERRY,
age eight

*"If a helicopter pilot's controls made contact with his rotors
as seldom as your poles make contact
with the snow, he'd crash."*
DAD

12

WHAT OTHER EQUIPMENT DOES A CHILD NEED?

Let's not go crazy with all the extra goodies you can get conned into buying. We've discussed goggles, hats, and mittens in their proper place—as clothing—which gets us down to the only three accessories you really need: poles, after-ski boots, and knapsacks.

Poles are the only strictly skiing item among the three, unless you also use them for supporting tomato plants or picking up paper. Personally, having watched lots of children on snow for a long time, I often wonder if poles are really necessary except as status symbols, but since most ski schools insist kids have them, you have to get them. However, they need not be the finest set of graphite sticks on the market.

What youngsters do need is an adequate pair for maybe $10 to $15, of the proper length (armpit height in the store), with breakaway handles (rather than those thumb-wrecking loops) and soft baskets. Scott makes a very good junior pole.

One model that interested me a couple of years ago at Las Vegas was a telescoping pair made by The Pole. Much like a camera tripod, the poles lengthen by having you loosen a nut, pull the pole down a notch, then retighten. This obviously accommodates growth for several seasons, which isn't a bad idea. However, I've found it hard to relock that nut so that it stays locked, and the pole is much weaker—prone to bend—that is a fixed-length pole. On balance, it's worked well enough for me to recommend it for casual skiers, but I'd be cautious if your children ski often.

One final point on poles: *the point.* Get rid of it. In the hands of an expert adult a sharp-pointed pole (increasingly rare) is dangerous; in the hands of a kid that arrowhead (not so rare, alas) can be lethal. Simply grind it down on a stone wheel, then hollow it with a drill, and notch it with a file. Simple to do and worth the effort.

After-ski boots speak for themselves, especially if you want the during-ski boots to last for two seasons. The purpose of an après-boot is to get your child from house to lodge (and back) without getting his socks wet or wearing out his ski boots. The boots should be lined, waterproof, high (about three inches higher than the deepest puddle he's apt to encounter), and ugly (so no one steals them). The best models are made from that rubberized gunk most army-navy stores sell. Their only problem, aside from sheer ugliness, is that they're warm enough to make feet perspire (and, therefore, to get socks wet), but this has an obvious solution: Take along another pair of socks for Junior to ski in. In any event, ignore fashion.

Knapsacks are Ullr's gift to the skiing parent, especially if you buy one properly. Their purpose is to teach a child discipline, self-reliance, and control and mastery of his equipment, which is a nice way of telling your child that he, not you, will carry his boots, goggles, extra mittens, spare socks, lip balm, and other miscellanea, as well as his skis and poles.

A good knapsack should have at least two pockets, one big enough for the boots and the other for the stuff you'd like to keep dry. It should also have adjustable straps because, unlike boots and skis and parkas, your child's knapsack shouldn't be outgrown in two seasons. This also means it should be big enough to carry the next size of ski boots he'll get. Finally, it should have another strap he can put around his stomach so it won't fall off his shoulders. Zippers on the small pocket(s) are a good idea (or else everything falls out), and the main (boot) pocket should have both a drawstring and a cover flap with another tiable string or buckle to give you an even-money chance of getting to the lodge and back again with both boots.

Valuable, though strictly optional, is a ski-and-pole carrier (like Ski Tote), which has the same character-building aspects as the knapsack. A carrier lets you pack the skis and poles together in one unit (*caveat:* make sure they work with the ski brakes!) that a youngster can carry either by the handle or over his shoulder with the strap; and then, best of all, they allow you to lock them to a tree or post. The worst that can happen is that he'll forget the combination—and he will, he will—but you should have it written down somewhere in your wallet (not on masking tape attached to the tote).

Some parents have written the combination on the back of an identification card–which all kids should carry—but that is only as secure as using masking tape on the tote: If your child loses the card, it points the finder right to the skis engraved with his name. Writing it on a separate piece of paper is akin to throwing it into the nearest snow pile, where it will end up after one use. Fortunately, I have found that after some length of time, accompanied by constantly repeated threats that "if you don't unlock it yourself you won't ski today; I'm not going to unlock it anymore ever again," Greg learned it. Then the lock broke and had to be replaced.

That's more than enough on clothing and equipment. Bring money. Skiing isn't a bargain-basement pastime.

Part III

Parents, Kids, and the Ski-school Experience

INTRODUCTION

Sometimes we get so worried about how far we still have to go in teaching kids to ski (Part IV), that we forget how far we've come since the mid-1970s. I remember Rudi Wyrsch—the Pied Piper of Mount Snow, the Big Tall Man on Skis who did more to popularize kids' programs than anyone in American ski history—fighting the reigning powers at the area just to survive. He fought for a piece of land on which to build his terrain garden (Piperville), fought to get it groomed, and fought to prevent its being mowed down after he finally got it built. Some seasons were better than others, but twice, as recently as the early 1970s, he saw Piperville reduced to rubble as the bulldozers rolled in. His successor, Tom Montemagni, has been far more fortunate and successful, largely because Rudi fought the war.

Today, instruction for young skiers is accepted as being important at most ski areas across the country, big as well as small. These programs are maybe 85 percent along the path that adult instruction has traveled, but when you consider that instruction in the United States is now formally conceded to be the best in the world—thanks to the 1979 international competition called Interski—that isn't bad. No one would flatten Piperville today, and when Mount Snow needed that site for a new lift it found a new locale for the terrain garden. While Part IV describes both the 85 percent we've traveled and the steps being taken to complete the remaining 15 percent, keep in mind that "things" aren't so bad these days.

For one thing, as we detail in Chapter 20, today's children's instructor is a professional in the accurate sense of the word. He's completed a prescribed course of study and passed examinations in both theory and practice, just as doctors and lawyers do. Getting those working papers from the Professional Ski Instructors of America (PSIA) isn't automatic, and I can name a few good skiers, even instructors, who haven't yet passed. I'm not about to say the PSIA manual is as thick or complex as United Airlines' for its pilots or the test quite so challenging as the New York State Bar exam, but the days of the ski school being the last resting place for has-been, down-and-out Austrian racers is finally ancient history. True, not all instructors are certified, anywhere, but the ratio is improving and this professionalism permeates the programs. In addition, both Montemagni and Bob Kunkel, who developed Copper Mountain's program, are former schoolteachers —and they're not the only ones.

Today's better-managed ski areas now also insist that the ski school become a "profit center" rather than a "service." Being one of those troglodytes who believes the profit motive breeds competence, I haven't been surprised to see the rapid improvement in teaching theory and method that accompanies this change in philosophy. Typically, when the Club Méditerranée announced its new program and facility for Copper Mountain, the release said firmly: "A Mini Club for youngsters, 4 –12 years of age, will be an important part of the resort. In a special section of the village, kiddies will enjoy daylong programs of sports, games, entertainment and excursions, geared to their interests and abilities. Children over 6 years of age will even have their own ski instructors and classes at the Club's Ski School." The reason? To make money for Club Med. Yet even earlier, Bob Kunkel had gotten better children's facilities and instructors by producing a profit. Believe it—the more money these programs make, the better they'll become—so don't look for any bargains when you sign your heir into school. The last thing you want is a cut-rate program.

The last hurdle to children learning how to ski has been jumped by the equipment and clothing manufacturers, as discussed in Part II. Thus, today, we've got well-clothed and well-equipped children enrolled in sophisticated, profit-making programs taught by certified professional instructors. Everything seems under control.

Except that life doesn't always work that way. For all the progress of late, we still have more than 700 ski areas in this country, and I'd still be hard-pressed to name fifty areas whose programs I respect. (Fifty is being generous.) For all the gains and breakthroughs, for all the propaganda in the brochures, most ski resorts remain mired in the muck of antiquity, afraid to break out lest they get cut off. At most areas, "gains" owe more to Montgomery than they do to Patton in inspiration and audacity.

Partly, this results from the fact that these modern techniques are quite new, and while they've proven themselves to be more effective on an objective basis since the mid-to-late-1970s, many old-line ski-school directors are understandably reluctant to abandon systems that have, to a greater or lesser degree, produced a generation of competent young American skiers. (Let's face it: Those advanced workshops for adult skiers have proven themselves to be a far more efficient teaching/learning tool than any traditional skiweek program, but you can still count the number of ski areas that offer good workshops on the fingers of two hands and still have enough fingers left over to type. If anything, children's instruction is gaining more quickly.)

But partly, as noted in Part I, parental dreams about and ambitions for their children present a serious problem for instructors and program directors that delays real progress. Being a parent, I share these anxieties and hopes, but being a professional ski-journalist, I also understand the situation from the instructor's viewpoint. "Of course I know a nine-year-old shouldn't be in our racing program," Montemagni has said several times, "but what can I do when Dad wants him to be and he's skiing well enough and I can't talk Dad out of it?" This, as the financial types say, is "the downside of the profit motive." Whatever Dad wants enough to pay for, Dad gets. (Montemagni has much more to say on this point, as we'll discuss in Chapter 16.)

Compounding this, Dad is almost certainly a skier himself, maybe even a good one, possibly armed with some technical knowledge, and conceivably a recent graduate of one of the excellent advanced-skier workshops for adults. So why shouldn't he feel free to interfere or point the way?

Simply this: I don't. Odds are I'm as good a skier as most parents, more technically knowledgeable because I've written about it so often and have been through a slew of these advanced-unto-fantasy workshops on assignment. Yet I let Montemagni and Kunkel, and the other instructors and directors, do their job with my kids. I won't even watch a class when Greg or Alix is in it (unless I'm thoroughly hidden from view), and I observe other classes only after I've received the permission of the director with the firm understanding that I don't interfere. In other words, I accept their professional competence.

But this doesn't mean you should abandon your children to the great faceless ski-teaching machine any more than you'd take one medical opinion on a serious illness. As parents, we have the responsibility to make sure our children are being taught properly (which is why my wife is active in the local PTA). That, however, means you must first learn something about ski instruction, then ask the right questions at the right time. Assuming you get to the area early enough—before ski-school shapeup begins—have no hesitation about asking the director what the school is teaching, how they're teaching it, and why. You want to know, either before or after the class, what that day's lesson is/was designed to do; that way, I can evaluate how well it worked when I ski with Greg or Alix afterward. (In this respect, I've learned to put less stock in what Greg and Alix tell me compared with what they show me on the hill.) Hopefully, Part IV will equip you with the questions to ask and the basis for making the evaluations. But you have to develop the discipline and restraint yourself.

Your children won't help you. As any of us know who've seen them explode out of regular school at 3 P.M. like bubbles from a bottle of soda, children look forward to going to *any* school with as much joy as adults have when contemplating a broken ankle. Going to school isn't what they have in mind for Saturday morning. The minute you show even the faintest willingness to listen to their complaints, you'll get a surfeit of the whimpers, whines, and cries. The only system I've found that works, that gets the kids to class willingly (all things in life being relative), is your firm commitment to their going. If you decide they're going to ski school every Saturday morning, they've got to go. No waffling, yielding, or abject submission.

You owe the ski school something else: verbal support. Believe me, I've challenged all manner of directors and instructors on theory and practice, and taken some to task in print; but I won't do it when Greg or Alix is around. The only time I'll tell Greg (Alix is still too young at five and a half) that what the instructor said is wrong is when I know Greg won't go back to that school. And even then I couch my criticism in adult euphemism by suggesting another school had a better idea.

Yet while you have the responsibility to monitor what your child is learning and to ask the director to explain whatever you think is wrong, be willing to listen to his answers. Whatever you may think, the tight-parallel turn is not the be-all/end-all of skiing, and amassing the fastest time through the gates is not the ultimate definition of best. For kids, having fun on skis— playing—is what the day on snow is all about. And in that sense, as Kunkel has often commented, maybe we adults can all learn from the children.

"... 'n' we made chocolate-chip cookies and those Froot Loop necklaces that give you special power . . ."
ALEXANDRA BERRY,
at age four and a half

13

HOW SHOULD YOU PICK A NURSERY?

Nurseries are a topic I often wish I could ignore, because all the good ones seem to violate more of the "rules" than they follow. You go to conferences and seminars and all the ski-school directors lay down fantasies about what a good nursery has to have. Then you ask your children which are the good nurseries and, believe it, the nurseries they pick haven't got all those good things the pros say they have to have. Some, like Judy Reiss's Valley Day School up Sugarbush way, come pretty close to meeting those objective criteria for excellence; but others, like Nancy Alfaro's little cubicle at Mount Snow, seem at first glance to offer little more than crowded chaos. But when the (chocolate) chips are down, Alix unhesitatingly picks Mount Snow's as the best, the only one she went to without a whimper of protest and still likes to visit on occasion, and it was the one Greg liked the best even during its anarchic pre-Sherburne days.

Overall, I think the same holds for ski schools and nurseries as for the larger education picture: What makes it work isn't the physical plant or the audiovisuals so much as the teacher and the director, and their sense of fun and commitment. Sure, all things being equal, it's nice to have a first-rate plant as well as a fine director, as Copper and Keystone as well as Sugarbush manage, but a good director is the more important element. That also explains why a slew of little ski areas you probably haven't heard of—places like Pat's Peak in New Hampshire's Monadnock region, to pick but one both my kids and I happen to like— do a fine job. They haven't got millions to spend on building a separate "fa-cility," but they sure take good care of the kids and let Mom and Pop ski relaxed. More important, they get the youngsters out on the snow as soon as they're ready, and begin the long process of producing their future clientele.

No one, over the decades, has done a better job of this than Bromley, which for all I know pioneered the modern ski nursery. It doesn't have the best plant in Vermont (although it's quite adequate), but when we started skiing, long before we had children, the word was around about what a good job Bromley did. It still does, even now that Stratton owns it. It takes and cares for infants (few others do) in a separate room; has a pleasant main room for the older children; allows all children to ski free until they're six; provides lessons for youngsters of any age who are ready and on-snow play for those who aren't. I've often suspected (who can prove this?) that many areas in Vermont have serious nursery/children's-ski-school programs only because Bromley was killing them with the parent trade.

What was interesting was how rival areas reacted. Mount Snow's initial reaction—when madcap Walt Schoenknecht owned the area and Rudi Wyrsch handled the kids' show—was colorful, capricious, and very chaotic. Then Killington took over and gave Tom Montemagni and Nancy Alfaro free hands (with tight purse strings) to impose order (and make money). Stratton's first pattern—it still basically holds—was to pretend it was Austria in the late 1930s. We'll have to watch the Stratton–Bromley merger of facilities carefully, although if anything, Stratton has a higher commitment to impeccable facilities and trappings and, on balance, is one of the most sophisticated resorts in the East. I just don't like its ski-school theory.

In recent years, ski nurseries across the nation have improved mightily, especially those that have been incorporated into the total children's ski-school program, which is where they belong. Areas and resorts still vary widely in the amount of direct control exercised by, and the interaction with, the director of the youth instruction programs, but most of the first- and second-line areas accept the concept that the nursery can no longer stand alone.

Fact is, occasionally, some areas integrate it too totally and stress the skiing too much at the expense of the nursery function. At Stratton, for instance, the nursery as I define it stops at the age of three. Children from four to six must take lessons, two a day if they stay the full day, and must use poles. (Austrian-theory ski schools generally seem to have a pole-plant fetish, but that's another story.) At the appointed time, all the little tykes line up outside the building and take a lesson, just as the grown-ups do, and when the lesson is over they go back inside. There's no attitude of "whether they want to or not" because, simply, there is no other option. Faced with this adult pressure, young children do as they're told, but it should surprise no one to learn that Stratton's was by far the quietest, most disciplined nursery I've seen. (Still, I have to admit it, Alix liked it even if it bothered me. Crank that fact into your equation; I pretend to no omniscience. And, let's face it—that Stratton program has produced some of the best downhill racers in America.)

Understand, I'm no advocate of laissez-faire education, as Greg can testify when I go over his homework. But skiing, like any sport, is play, and when any area of play is regimented too much, the spontaneous joy and the chance for personality development and exploration go with it. Skiing becomes, instead, another unpleasant product of the adult world, and some children begin to cringe as soon as they see the flags and the base lodge. The teenage son of good friends of ours told me recently he hated to go skiing when he was a child because the lessons were so bad—"too adult," he phrased it.

Skiing should be something the child does when he's ready. If for any reason a four-year-old (or, for that matter, a fourteen-year-old) doesn't feel like skiing that day, he should have other valid options provided by the ski area at its nurseries. At the same time, the nursery should be designed and planned so that it inexorably pushes a child toward *wanting* to learn how to ski. Some of the games should be subtly aimed at teaching children something about equipment, so that when they are finally ready to ski the on-snow instructor doesn't have to waste half his class time buckling boots and checking bindings.

This, however, is a difficult goal to meet, and few areas really meet all facets of it. At one end of the spectrum is the Stratton program; at the other end, and far the more typical, is the babysitting/day-care-center solution, where skiing (and playing in the snow generally) is ignored. Many areas—including some of the best on other criteria—still have no provision for a child's taking a lesson as part of its nursery program (your decision as a parent is limited to either/or), which I feel is far worse than the Stratton solution.

Fortunately, many of the better ski resorts have begun to develop a good middle ground, where lessons are offered on a casual basis to those little children who want them, but where the devout nonskier can still have fun and not be ostracized or rejected. Typically, these nurseries are run by two or three full-time people, who split the group into skiers and nonskiers —in a constantly shifting shuffle—and who accommodate each subgroup well. "We occasionally have some children as old as nine and ten who don't want to ski," said the head of the excellent Keystone program, "and they're more than welcome here. We always have something for them to do. Why should anyone be forced to ski, no matter how old he is?" Or, why should he be forced to sit in the base lodge if he doesn't want to ski?

How do you find these middle-ground areas? I could list a group of maybe twenty for you, but it wouldn't be anywhere near complete, and, besides, what was good one season can change within the next two. Instead, let's examine the basic criteria of what a good nursery program should have:

* *Ski lessons available.* Sometimes I think Mount Snow carries this to a pleasant extreme, and a few times Alix was a class of one. The way this generally works is that sometime between 9:30 and 10:30 (varies from area to area, and often month to month depending on the weather), the supervisor announces that those who want lessons should start dressing (putting on all the clothing they just took off), buckling boots, and the like. Those who don't want lessons continue finger-painting or making Froot Loop necklaces or whatever; the others saddle up and go outside. The lessons are held close to the nursery itself (a major qualification, since four-year-olds quickly get tired walking) and tend to be rudimentary, rarely more advanced than learning a primitive wedge-turn or wedge-stop. After about an hour, the class clumps back in, undresses, and begins to play again. The lesson usually costs a few bucks more than the nursery-only program, but if the child is willing, it's well worth the money. The point is, it's both casual and available, and the major nursery activities—like making cookies or fondue—are done after the lesson. . . . However, nursery lessons can only go so far. In January 1980, Alix asked to return to the Mount Snow nursery and take a lesson, so of course we agreed. But when we gathered Alix up at 2 P.M., Nancy and the instructor told us that Alix had become too good a skier for lessons there, and from now on, it was ski-school-only. Alas, another graduation.

* *Pleasant games.* A ski-school nursery should be as advanced as a preschool nursery, or even a kindergarten. It should offer many of the same types of nonskiing programmed activities: good toys and games, finger-painting, story-reading sessions. Many of the better ski nurseries are run by people who've been teachers, which is unquestionably an advantage, al-

though if the director is a prison-matron type, forget it.

* *Pleasant Environment.* This speaks for itself on the obvious level: A nursery should be attractive and colorful and filled with playthings, and if it looks like a prison cell it probably is. Chaos is preferable to too much order. However, other qualifications emerge: Does the nursery tie into the ski area and the ski experience? Can the child look out of a window and see people skiing, milling around, or walking by in ski clothing? Does it have a door leading easily out to the ski-lesson terrain? Even some of the best fail in this department, but there has been progress. Many areas now realize they can't use the old boiler room much longer.

* *Separate facilities.* Ideally, each child should have his own locker/box/hook, a place to store his equipment and clothing so that he can find them easily at lesson or lunch time. However, this, too, is still in the idealized stage at many resorts, so writing your child's name on the mittens and skis and all like that is mandatory. (That's pretty good advice even if the area does have separate boxes.)

* *Lunch facilities.* This is a two-headed qualification, thanks to my wife, who suggests strongly that you should look for a nursery that has tables. These allow the youngsters to have a good surface to play games on as well as eat. More important to me, however, is the fact of having food itself; a good nursery should have its own kitchen (at least a refrigerator), because otherwise the children may have a long wait if the cafeteria backs up.

* *Infant facilities.* Depending on state laws and resort policies, some ski areas will accept infants; most won't.

As a rule, those that do are licensed by the state and must comply with staffing, health, and other requirements, which tends to make the whole operation better. However, make sure the infant room is separate from the general nursery, and that the older children can't drift into and out of it easily. Areas that don't take infants usually set as a minimum requirement that the child be past the age of diapers.

Finally, don't keep popping in and out to check on your child. It wrecks the discipline and flow of a program. Treat the nursery as you would a real live school—because that's what it is.

"*I pressed the area management to price the children's lessons the same as the adults': thirteen dollars for a full day, nine dollars for half day. That took a lot of convincing but since my costs are the same as the adult school's, and since we pay our instructors the same salary, why shouldn't we charge the same price? We've had no resistance from the parents.*"

BOB KUNKEL,
reflecting a policy that's become common
in the Rockies and is growing elsewhere

"*We're in the service business.*"
TOM MONTEMAGNI

14

HOW SHOULD YOU PICK
A SKI SCHOOL?

Ski areas are businesses, and ski schools should be profit
centers; yet as many of us know, it wasn't always thus. Go back
even ten years and few industries had better claim to the old
gag, "We're not organized as a not-for-profit corporation, it just
works out that way." Any ski area that saw more than a 5
percent profit on revenue (forget return-on-investment) was
drummed out of the club. Ski schools at best were regarded as
"services" the area provided, and every director had at least a
bronze medal from some obscure race in Europe and an accent
to match, neither of which qualified him to teach or plan an
instruction program. Ski-area management in short was a mess,
and instruction was usually worse; that was probably how
things were when today's adults learned how to ski.

Those days, fortunately, are going quickly. When big and
mid-sized national corporations like Ralston Purina, Goliad
Oil, and Solon Automated Industries got into the ski game, they
brought some radical ideas with them, such as that their invest-
ments were supposed to generate a real profit. They went down
the line, service by service, and decided that some subsystems
were supposed to make their own profit also. Thus were born
the professional ski-school director, the instructor, and the program. (PSIA has another version. Trust mine.)

Today, if you want your children to get a good ski-school
education, you're going to pay for it; if the area persists in giving
it away cheap, that's what it's worth. Bob Kunkel, in fact,
would prefer to charge more for children's lessons than for
adults', because the work is the same and the challenges more

141

profound. Also, he says, "If you charge more, you can pay your instructors more and get the best. If you get the best, you can demand the most from them. If they produce a good product, it sells itself and your reputation for quality goes up. That way, you can make a good profit, which gives you bargaining power with upper management."

As a result of even the current equal-pay/charge policy, you now have the right to expect more. You have the right to insist on seeing something for your money, on getting intelligent answers (certainly courtesy) from instructors and directors, on being shown a total program and network of facilities designed to produce good young skiers. A children's program should be every bit as formal and structured in organization as the adult versions, and you should get annoyed if it isn't.

Let's get specific about what to look for:

* *A totally integrated program,* from nursery school through junior racing and freestyle. One person should have control over all "junior" facilities, and be able to move children from nursery to ski school to advanced programs when and if the youngster is ready, willing, and able. The nursery school's instructors should be part of the area's school. For corporate administration, most areas still put the junior program under the adult ski-school system; others are beginning to split it off as a separate unit. This really doesn't matter, just so long as the junior program is a totally contained unit.

    As a corollary, youngsters should *never* be put into an adult class. No ifs, ands, buts, qualifications, or exceptions. Never. The good resorts and areas have, or are creating, special programs for teenagers, such as Vail's "Teen Connection," while others have classes or season-long sessions for experts not interested in racing, such as Pat's Peak's or Waterville Valley's junior-instructor programs.

* *A distinct, articulate philosophy of teaching.* All directors and instructors must be able to explain what they teach, what their objectives are/were for that class that day and how those fit into the overall program/ syllabus/progression. An increasing number of areas have produced mimeographed syllabi or progressions; don't be shy about asking for one. (See Copper Mountain's in the Appendix.)

* *Proper facilities.* These should include separate nursery quarters, lift, and terrain garden (see below), hopefully located close to the main base lodge; but many excellent programs operate with far less. If nothing else, the absence of facilities puts some pressure on the director to explain how his school works wonders without them. However, any area can, and should, have a separate meeting place for youngsters, lest they get lost amid the chaos of the adult "shapeup."

* *A complement of men instructors* on the kids' staff. That's not a male chauvinist comment. Men are neither better nor worse at teaching children how to ski; as always, it depends on the competence of the particular instructor. The presence of men suggests that the area takes its program seriously enough to pay the same salaries for teaching children as it does for adults. For far too long, the ski-school director's incumbent girlfriend got the kiddies' job, and it's nice to have some demonstrable evidence that the particular area has changed that orientation in favor of professionalism.

* *A fair ratio of "certified" instructors* on the staff. I can't think of any ski school in which all instructors have their PSIA "badges"—meaning they passed even the first level of their certification exams—but

all schools have some who have. The ratio changes depending on many factors irrelevant to this book, but a parent does have the right to expect that the children's program should have roughly the same ratio of certified instructors as the adult program. The degree of disparity—and some will exist any-where—will tell you how seriously the ski area takes its junior programs. It's true, as Tom Montemagni notes, that the exam doesn't test for proficiency in teaching children and that a separate exam should be required, but it's not about to happen that way for a while and we must live with the current certification as some indication, albeit imperfect, that the area cares.

* *Flexibility of scheduling.* This is a touchy point that can be argued either way, but I feel a children's ski school should be able to accommodate half-day as well as full-day students. (This is the one major facet of the SKIwee program I'm unhappy with.) Sure, some youngsters are delighted to hit the area and spend the full weekend in class with their friends (new or old), and a lot of parents are thrilled at the prospect. But some children like to ski with their parents, and some parents with their children. Also, some youngsters are as susceptible as adults to the weekend syndrome, and are willing to compromise on one two-hour class over the weekend but please, no more school, it's time to play, free of any regimentation or instruction, even from a program as play-oriented as SKIwee. The pro-gram should be able to live with that.

Terrain gardens are one subject on which everyone waffles: If you have one, you insist it's mandatory; if you don't, you treat it as irrelevant, excessive, coddling, etc. I think that a good terrain garden is a major advantage, but you're apt to run into a bad facility as easily as a good one.

A terrain garden is not just a group of pretty cutout Snoopys and a couple of lengths of sewer pipe. That's a playground, but all too often that's what a ski area means when it says it has a terrain garden. A terrain garden should be an organized, planned selection of physical challenges isolating specific skiing problems, reduced to a compact, child-scale section; and like the ballpark in baseball's rule book, it should be enclosed. (It should also have its own lift, but that's a nice "extra," not mandatory.) It may also have pretty cutout Snoopys or balloons to add spice and color, but what makes it work are the selected drills and the skills the facilities develop.

Properly designed, a terrain garden will make children learn how to make a turn at a specific place, how to adjust to changes in terrain (pitch, bumps), how to transfer weight from one ski to another, how to use a flat ski or an edge, and how to stop. It provides one place to climb and run straight, and other places to learn other sensations of weighting and steering and banking. It is, in short, a precise teaching machine, and as such has to be designed well and located on the right piece of terrain. It also has to be groomed regularly and properly. Some designers use haybales, others bulldozers, to create the various facilities, but if they're not maintained during the season they quickly become worthless.

How can you tell if the garden will help your child's skiing grow? How can you tell if Snoopy's the decoration that makes the drill facility work, or if it's the whole thing? No firm guideline exists as to what a terrain garden should have, but a few rudiments date back to the late 1960s, when Vail and Mount Snow began pushing into this area:

* *"Pedal" or "bicycle" track.* You create two tracks, each wide enough for only one ski (or else the kids cheat), with alternating bumps and valleys. Viewed from the front, the child is lifting one ski and pushing the other one down, just as if he were riding a bike.

* *"Waterfall"* or *"washboard."* This can be quite wide, to the point that several children can ski it abreast. It moves from flats to drops to flats to drops, with a long flat outrun so that a beginner can use it without knowing how to stop. It resembles a small-scale series of ridgelines of the type you'll meet on many mountains. It accustoms children to changes in terrain.

* *"Bob"* or *"luge"* track. As it sounds, it's a U-shaped run, preferably with bends (for turns) built into a pair of high walls. It resembles a lot of catwalks, and must be high and gentle enough to allow the child to bank through his turns without actually making a turning maneuver. It accustoms a child to the fact that he is supposed to turn, and will actually turn the skis for the skier who can't.

* *Race course.* Obviously, we're not talking about the SL run on Whiteface, but a good terrain garden has a series of slalom poles (usually decorated with balloons or colored cutouts) for the more advanced kids to turn around. It accustoms a child to making turns at specific times and places, rather than just when he feels like it.

* *Bumps, moguls, cones, jumps.* See Glossary.

To me, the existence of a good terrain garden—like the publication of a progression/syllabus—suggests I'm dealing with a first-line, professional operation. The absence of one doesn't suggest the opposite, but one question should be asked: "Why not?" The more of this type of indication you see, the more you can relax and leave your children in school with confidence. These are the waves of the future, so ask for them. If enough people ask . . .

Photo courtesy of Indianhead Mountain, Wakefield, Michigan.

"For the first three days of the Centered Skiing workshop, my skiing disintegrated, spiraling downward until I considered quitting forever."
I. WILLIAM BERRY,
three days into a five-day seminar for advanced skiing

"So the instructor said that since we had icy moguls we should learn how to ski icy moguls, and he took us up on Ciao . . ."
"But that's an expert trail."
"Right, and we went up there and he showed us how to ski icy moguls and we lost one of the kids . . ."
"You lost one of the kids?"
"Right, and we went looking for him while we were skiing icy moguls and we had the most fun."
"Terrific."
DIALOGUE
between Gregory Berry, nine, and Dad, suddenly aged ninety-nine, after Greg's lesson at Waterville Valley and before Dad learned "lost child" was the instructor's teaching gimmick

"What did you learn today?"
"Nothin'. Let's go skiing."
GREG,
after most lessons

15

HOW CAN YOU EVALUATE A SKI-SCHOOL LESSON?

How does a parent evaluate the results of one two-hour lesson? You don't. Maybe it's that simple. Maybe we ought to move on to the next chapter.

Still, you're not about to be satisfied with that answer. You've just laid out $5 to $10 to put your child into class, you've seen him run the gantlet of the ski-off and head into the hills with the guy wearing the red-white-and-blue lacquered pin that says he's a professional instructor, and you've come back two hours later to collect Killy Jr. and wait for the verdict. "Nothin'." Terrific. Gimme my money back.

Problem is, adults are programmed to get something for their money. Something demonstrable. *We* go into class—trauma enough—and that instructor better lay something heavy on us or we're gonna scream. So he watches us take a run and he says, "Your left hand is coming up too high and then falling back, which is why you're losing your carve halfway through the turn and that's enough for eight bucks so go practice." We're happy. But kids happen to be smarter, so they reply, "Which is my left hand?"

As we know, skiing is a complex sport involving intricate eye-hand-foot coordination; a turn is a subtle maneuver. No one can teach all aspects in one lesson; the Sugarbush workshop takes nine two-hour lessons just to teach all facets of making a specialized carved turn to already strong advanced skiers (after which you spend all season trying to *learn* it). Early in that sequence, your skiing really disintegrates as they remove

149

one bad-habit crutch after another, a necessary preliminary to teaching good movements that, hopefully, will become the new habits in time. So how do you evaluate the Tuesday morning or Wednesday afternoon lesson in that sequence?

Children are no different. As you read through the Copper syllabus in the Appendix, you'll begin to see how carefully the movements are broken down into "subsystems" or secondary subskills, and how crucial it is on occasion to let a youngster "free-ski" for two hours with just one helpful hint from the instructor. At some point in a sequence of lessons, the whole thing comes together and the skier leaps forward to a new plateau, but you wouldn't be justified in assuming that that lesson was the good one any more than you would that the "building lessons" were bad. That's why, as I mentioned earlier, you have to question the instructor.

In fact, during some years, I "learned" best during the summer. Early in March 1979, for instance, I took a couple of days of refresher instruction at Sugarbush, and Martin Marnett (a superb instructor) had added a few refinements to the workshop since I'd last visited. He'd created a concept of "leading the turn by letting your hip fall down the hill." Take it on faith, there is no way you're going to grasp that immediately. I took it with me on my western swing, thought about it, tried it, forgot it. It was hopeless—until the following November, when somehow it came together the second day out. It had touched a subtle nerve all summer long; I caught myself thinking about it in random moments and, finally, it began to work when I got back on snow. Sometimes.

This tendency is even more marked with children, who have the added advantage of continuing to grow and mature on all levels at an incredible if uneven speed. Between November and March they get an awesome amount of new things tossed at them about skiing—probably too much—but between March and November some of it filters out and the other parts remain and somehow, the first or second day back on skis, the whole essence of last season falls in. This is one reason I'm in no hurry to put Greg into ski school early in the season.

But this phenomenon doesn't generate an immediate, discernible return on your investment. Ski-school directors know this, and some of the more pragmatic, sales-oriented types invent names for maneuvers taught that day. "We tell the kids," Bob Kunkel has said, "to tell Dad they just learned a 'gorilla' or 'banana' turn. Sure it's a bit silly, but what else can we do? Most parents just don't understand the mechanics of teaching and learning, so we have to give them something they can take with them. Like a 'banana turn.' "

This occasionally produces real nonsense, like the famed "airplane turn." More than one—a lot more than one—instructor has commented that even a good skier can't make one because the arms and hips go the wrong way if you "bank the plane" properly; yet some schools still teach them, as part of the sales progression, and many parents are happy when their child comes back and says, "I learned the 'airplane turn.' "

It is important to understand that children and adults don't look at ski lessons, or ski schools, the same way on still another level. Where "real people" see the peril in skiing, kids see the fun. The idea that that Waterville instructor would take an "E" class onto steep, icy moguls made me turn pale beneath my tan. *I* hesitated to ski that trail that day, but to Greg it was fun, one of the lessons he talked about for the rest of the season and well into the summer. Not surprisingly, a class venture onto the equally expert Jaws of Death at Mount Snow under even more marginal conditions was another well-remembered episode on his season's-best list. I still think both instructors were nuts, but Greg disagrees . . . and I must admit he seemed to have learned more from those lessons (in addition to raw survival) than from the saner ones.

This is not a random thought, and it should make you very cautious about rating lessons and ski schools. You must learn how to evaluate them through your child's eyes, not your own, and probably the best way to do that is to watch as the other youngsters come down at the end of a class. If they're happy and excited, just bursting with things to show and tell, that's a good ski school—or at least, that class had a good instructor. If a whole series of classes come down that way, the school as well as the instructor is good.

Your child should have fun skiing, and if skiing isn't fun, tear it up and try something else— or, more to the point, try another ski school at another area. And make sure the area's management knows why you're changing.

Finally, ask for an appraisal of how well your child is skiing and learning. It's a very normal question to ask, one I often ask myself. Perhaps, in the course of a ninety-minute Saturday-morning lesson where he's had nine kids under his wing, the instructor may not have been able to teach much; but he should have been able to size up your child. A good question to follow with is, where can he ski, and where shouldn't he ski? (For obvious reasons, this whole sequence should be discussed out of the child's hearing— especially that business about where he can ski—because once he knows he's gotten the instructor's go-ahead on black diamonds, you're sunk.)

Purgatory, Colorado. Photo by John Briner.

"Dr. Richard Steadman, director of the U.S. Ski Team's medical staff, gave the following report on each of the athlete's rehabilitation programs. . . . Three screws were removed from his *ankle. . . . Surgery repairs were made on torn medial collateral ligaments and anterior cruciate ligaments of the right knee and medial collateral repair to* her *left knee from previous injury. Both casts were removed. . . . Dr. Steadman has removed all screws from* her *knees, but she will continue to wear a brace. . . ."*

ROUTINE CASUALTY REPORT
in a press release from the U.S. Ski Team office
in Park City, Utah, 21 September 1979

"The Little League Syndrome, with parents screaming at the kids to win, is a disgrace. I've seen kids turn pale and vomit before a race, and parents who ignore their kids afterwards if they lose."

DR. DON OVEREND

"The purpose of the competition program is first and foremost to raise the level of skiing. Secondly, it is to have fun: Ski racing is an experience that should be enjoyed. And if the kids win a race here and there, that's gravy."

WES HAIGHT,
head coach of Mount Snow's ski team

"That raised a few eyebrows when my new head coach [Wes] said that to the Mount Snow Ski Club, but we've stuck to that philosophy for the past two years."

TOM MONTEMAGNI

16

WHEN SHOULD A CHILD START RACING?

The question of ski racing is a difficult and controversial subject, the one on which the initial draft of this book drew the most comment from the experts and the chapter that bothered me the most. So I researched the topic anew and, for a short time, put Greg into the best young-racer program I could find, the highly developed and sophisticated Educational Foundation at Pat's Peak, New Hampshire, where we've skied for years. This small but beautifully run ski area in the state's Monadnock region—near Vermont and Massachusetts—manages, year after year, to produce as many good racers as giant Waterville Valley; its program is every bit as professional as the more famous ones at Burke and Stratton, Vermont, and more success-oriented than the one at Mount Snow. Were the area not located close to my house in New Hampshire, I could have chosen equally good programs at such other small areas as West and Willard Mountains in New York or Jiminy Peak in the Berkshires. As an overall rule, in fact, if you're deeply committed to having your children race, these small areas do every bit as good a job as the giants, and usually for a lot less money.

But do you want your child to race? And if so, at what age?

Essentially, I'm opposed to it before a youngster hits twelve, and I have reservations even then. This feeling antedates my having children, being married, or even skiing; one of my first acts as a professional newsman more than two decades ago was to replace a vacationing sports editor in eastern

Pennsylvania and write a three-part series excoriating the parental pressures in Little League baseball. (Not too long afterward, I was working in Ohio, Woody Hayes country, which oddly tolerated disagreement over sports philosophy more than the Poconos did.) Having children has, if anything, hardened my opposition to the "Little League Syndrome." If neither Greg nor Alix decides to race in anger, that's fine with me.

At the same time, I appreciate what racing *training* can do for a good young skier: It will make him a better recreational skier. Take some nine- or ten-year-old skier who's comfortable just lazing down the hill with a highly controlled skid-and-rebound technique and a minimum of effort (or turns), put him into a racing program, and he'll suddenly find his edge and an appreciation of the best "line" down the hill. (Problem is, once he finds that he'll blow you off the hill—but that's life.)

So, what do you do with a good, strong young skier? If you deprive him of a good racing clinic you will, I feel, limit his growth as a skier; if you put him into one, you may ensnare him in psychological problems he can't handle—not to mention exposing yourself to that same pressure (and no, none of us is immune). It's something to think about seriously.

If you're talking about big-time racing, culminating at the U.S. Ski Team level, my answer is, don't do it. Stay away from that whole U.S. Ski Association/Ski Educational Foundation rat race. Halfbacks in the NFL have a better chance of walking normally when their careers are done. Youngsters get killed in downhill practice sessions; one young star on the Italian National Team was in a coma for more than a year after a crash at Lake Placid during the 1979 pre-Olympics. Slalom and giant-slalom skiers do terrible things to their ankles and knees as they seek the outer limits of physical durability. Billy Kidd and Phil Mahre, two of the top racers the United States has produced, have logged almost as much time in casts and rehabilitation programs as they have on the course, and they are among the best. Racers at a lower ability level suffer just as much physical damage—Tiania Tutt, a former Ski Team member who wisely decided to abandon it in favor of college, was badly injured in a minor downhill race in Colorado in 1980—without the compensating financial rewards of the handful of first-liners. I can show you issues of *Ski Racing* in which full pages are devoted to "progress reports" on the walking wounded.

True, recreational skiing is a potentially dangerous sport— as we discuss in the next chapter—but although the statistics are remarkably unsophisticated for the 1980s, the chances of getting hurt *seriously* seem to have declined to less than one per 1,000 skier days. It's also true, as Tom Montemagni comments, that we have few valid statistics about injuries in competition, but as I write, I am hard-pressed to name many members of the current U.S. Ski Team who haven't had at least a serious sprain or torn ligament in the recent past.

Is it worth it? I guess my answer would be this: If your child wants to race at that level so badly he's willing to fight you to do it, then maybe you should go along with it. But even then, you should remain a low-key moderating force, never trying to push him beyond what he's doing, never chastising him for failure, and letting him know he can always come home again without a gold medal.

If there's one place you probably should push, though, it's on schooling. As a quick rule (we can name the few exceptions easily), youngsters who give up college to venture onto the World Cup circuit (as they usually must) find themselves discarded by the coaches and establishment (and all too often by the industry) in their early twenties with no career, no viable skills (the business world isn't snowed by the ability to make a carved turn), and little to hope for, aside from a hanger-on slot as a manufacturer's sales representative while the good jobs within skiing go to the bright new lights carrying MBAs and LLBs on their resumes.

A few—the Phil Mahres, Billy Kidds, and Hank Kashiwas —make a decent income during their peak years and parlay their success and personalities into decent post-racing contracts. Shrewd ones like Tom Corcoran even go back and get their degrees and do well in the ski industry. That accounts for maybe 1 percent of the serious American racers (the European scene is totally different). I suspect the parents of the other 99 percent have had some sleepless nights wondering if they did the right thing when they played racer-chaser, because somewhere back in that racer's youth his folks said sure, go for it.

This doesn't mean your child shouldn't race, such as taking an occasional run through the NASTAR gates or, if he's been skiing a few years and is about to enter his teens, even signing up for a junior racing program at the ski area you visit regularly. That's fine, if that's what he wants. But above all, keep a sense of proportion: Ski-racing isn't the be-all/end-all of life, or even of skiing.

Racing classes do have one advantage: Properly supervised, they teach the ultimate in ski technique and control. They also, for the teenager, provide a needed challenge and extension of the ski experience until he's old enough to find the real challenge of the sport within himself (which is, admittedly, an adult process). In addition, the better programs include freestyle (ballet and mogul maneuvers) in the "racing" classes, and a ski-area program that offers ballet, mogul-mashing, and giant-slalom racing is going to produce an excellent recreational skier—as long as it doesn't get out of control.

One control factor is the program director. Tom Montemagni, commenting about the father who wants his son to race when the youngster isn't ready yet, said: "This is why I changed the program to include working on high-level skill development that will prepare them for the time they can handle real competition. In the meantime, [they learn] smooth GS turning, riding an edge, fast skiing under control, and recognizing and handling different terrain situations."

What about the youngster who wants and needs to compete? "We can't deny them a chance," Montemagni says firmly. "But the program must allow for individual differences, and the coaches must understand the extent of the physical abilities of the different age groups and individuals and how much competition the kids want and can handle. And always, we must focus on the goals we set in saner moments before the season began."

Like Mount Snow's, Pat's Peak's program keys on trying to fit the youngster into different slots along the competition ladder, and each racer is rated on the detailed form included at the end of this chapter. "If the coaches don't feel a youngster is ready for tough competition, physically or emotionally, we won't put him into the regional and state-level races," says Elliot Snow, who runs the under-thirteen group. "We'll keep him down at the Buddy Werner League level, which is much lower keyed. We'll also," he adds, "keep irate parents off the backs of the coaches who made the decision."

Still, the biggest control factor is the parent. If you really think that winning some race run by the U.S. Ski Association is important, your child will too, and worse, he's going to feel terrible when he loses. (Most children do lose, you know.) Fathers, says Dr. Don Overend, are the worst offenders, especially those fathers who never quite "made it" as athletes. "If you don't get it under control," he warns, "you'll ruin not only racing but skiing itself for your kids."

The beauty of racing, if you let your children hang out and just enjoy it, is that it's a natural episode. Whenever I turn Greg loose to go off and ski by himself, he immediately finds another kid and bang, off they go in a seemingly endless series of races, lickety-split down the easy slope, and he's as apt to say "He was better" as "I was better" with no feeling of inadequacy; the episode was its own reward. When he entered his first children's NASTAR at the age of eight, he was pleased he finished (itself an accomplishment) in the middle of the pack because I was pleased—and as a result, he had fun racing.

Just as important, he learned something about skiing by running those gates, because for the first time he had to make his turns in a specific place. (Just the fact that he had to make turns was important.) He also had to be setting his edges; an eight-year-old won't finish in the middle by skidding all the way down. Finally, he learned something important about terrain and taking a correct line, which can be hard to teach.

The following year, in his once-a-season gambol through the gates, he had even more fun by winning a NASTAR gold medal on an easy course. Whether it was the early-season classes in race-training, or the concentrated three-day SKIwee program right before the race, or just a general maturing, I don't know; but by watching how he came through the course you could see how much he'd improved as a *skier* in just one year.

At the same time, I'd hate to see him race too often, even just for fun, because racing, at too young an age, can develop as many bad habits as good. (Just watch me to see how badly a good recreational skier can ski in the gates.) The most important bad habit to watch for in young skiers (below age twelve) is what the racing coaches note: a failure to complete one turn before moving on to the next turn. They fail to run through the natural sequence and flow of a turn because (1) they haven't fully learned how yet, (2) the gates come at them faster than their reaction times can handle, and (3) the course is set on too steep a piece of terrain. If they do this too long and too often, they never quite learn how to finish a turn, even though their ever-increasing leg strength and ability to initiate a turn compensate. Essentially, they learn how to skate rather than ski, which can be counterproductive in skiing deep powder.

Most authorities—pediatricians, racing coaches, *et al.*— believe the solution to that problem is two-fold: (1) Run all kids through giant-slalom, rather than the far tighter slalom, courses to give them more time to make each turn; and (2) don't allow kids into the racing programs much before they're twelve. "The Europeans have come to the same conclusion," says Sigi Grottendorfer, head of the Sugarbush, Vermont, and Portillo, Chile, ski schools. "Children have to know how to *ski* well before they can *race* well."

"We have two problems with the last solution," Tom Montemagni says bluntly. "Kids and parents. Maybe the real problem has been ski schools," he admits on second thought, "because until recently we haven't known what to do with a good young skier, maybe as young as eight or nine, who's skiing at the 'F' class level and is getting bored. Maybe he's a fine natural athlete as well, so we've put him in the racing program.

"These days, though, we've begun to create different forms of advanced-skiing programs for kids." (Waterville Valley was probably the pioneer, although I wouldn't be surprised to learn that some small area I've never visited antedated Waterville by five years.) "We've created our 'Demonstration Class' for the stronger skiers, where we do a lot of controlled free skiing, often on some difficult trails, and we work on some racing, some freestyle, some mountain lore and nature lessons." This, he says, keeps the kids learning and progressing. Other areas are using children as junior hosts and hostesses or junior patrolmen, functions that get them involved in the mountain and with other skiers. (After all, why shouldn't the patrolman become as good a "role image" as the racer?) Still others, like Pat's Peak, create a junior-ski-instructor program for strong teenagers who don't want to race.

"But even those programs," Montemagni says, "don't solve the problem of the father who wants his kid to race. What do you do then?"

The best way to answer that is to report that Phil Mahre (and his twin brother, Steve) didn't start racing until he was twelve. Mahre is unquestionably the best World Class racer the United States has ever produced (including Kidd, the Cochran girls, and Cindy Nelson), and he offers the following advice (in an article a few years ago in *Young Athlete*):

"A lot of kids are into skiing [racing] to win, win, win when they're only kneehigh to a grasshopper. When they get older they get tired of that pace and pressure. Pretty soon, they're not having any fun at all and they quit. . . . You [shouldn't] let anyone pressure you. You have to make your own decisions. I think a lot of parents pressure their kids into doing something; that's all wrong because the kids will usually rebel instead of succeeding."

I'd hate to tell you how many potentially fine racers who started younger were burned out by the time they were seventeen. That isn't physical; that's psychological.

No convenient, all-encompassing solution exists. Parents and children are different, of course, and we all have different values. To me, skiing's advantage over most sports is that it's a lifetime pastime—provided the knees and ankles still work, and provided you have a career that generates enough income to be able to afford to pursue this increasingly expensive addiction. That's your choice to make for your young child, because at ten he can't make it for himself. The following is Pat's Peak form for evaluating potential young racers. Don't infer I approve of all the implicit values; some of those under "Aggression" and "Responsibility," for instance, aren't traits I want Greg or Alix to develop. But this is the form that the directors of one of the best racing programs in the country have designed.

PATS PEAK EDUCATIONAL FOUNDATION
HENNIKER, N.H.

RACER EVALUATION

NAME_____AGE_____DATE_____

TECHNICAL EVALUATION

                                    weak   adequate   strong

Natural and relaxed body
    position   _____

Effective use ankle & knee
    angulation   _____

Mid-body coordination _____

Upper body stance/arm
    & hand function   _____

Correct use of line   _____

      Short radius   _____

      Long radius   _____

Special aids (orthodics, cants, boot modification, forward lean,
boot height, heel height)_____
_____
_____

General Comments:_____
_____
_____
_____
_____

PHYSICAL EVALUATION

                                      weak   adequate   strong

Flexibility   _____

Strength   _____

Stamina   _____

Coordination   _____

Quickness/reaction speed _____

Balance   _____

Competitive instincts   _____
Overall attitude
  (are they motivated?)   _____
Aggressiveness   _____
Self-confidence   _____
Visual perception   _____
Equal ability right and left   yes__no_____
specify_____
_____
_____

Physical disabilities (weak ankles, knee, etc.) yes__no_____
specify_____
_____
_____

General Comments:_____
_____
_____
_____
_____

CAMP_____COACH_____
RATING: (1) low, (2) below average, (3) average, (4) above average, (5) high

Drive. Desires to win or be successful; aspires to accomplish difficult tasks; sets and maintains high goals for himself in athletics; responds positively to competition; desires to attain athletic excellence; willing to do unpleasant things if he thinks they will help him.   1/2/3/4/5

Aggression. Believes one must be aggressive to win; releases aggression easily; enjoys confrontation and argument; sometimes willing to use force to get his way; will not allow others to push him around; may seek to "get even" with people whom he perceives as having harmed him.   1/2/3/4/5

Determination. Willing to practice long and hard; works on skills until exhausted; often works out willingly by himself; perseveres, even in the face of great difficulty; is patient and unrelenting in his work habits; doesn't give up quickly on a problem.   1/2/3/4/5

Responsibility. Accepts responsibility for his actions; accepts blame and criticism even when not deserved; tends to dwell on his mistakes and to punish himself for them; willing to endure much physical and mental pain; will ski even when injured.   1/2/3/4/5

Leadership. Enjoys the role of leader and may assume it spontaneously; believes others see him as a leader; attempts to control his environment and to influence or direct other people; expresses opinions forcefully; usually good at getting what he wants from others.   1/2/3/4/5

Self-confidence. Very sure of himself and his ability; confident of his ability to deal with things; handles unexpected situations well; makes decisions confidently; not prone to worry about his play or to show indecisiveness; speaks up for his beliefs to coaches and players.   1/2/3/4/5

Emotional Control. Tends to be emotionally stable and realistic about athletics; is not easily upset; will rarely allow his feelings to show and his performance is not affected by them; not easily depressed or frustrated by bad breaks, calls, or mistakes; a great deal of self-discipline is evident in this person's behavior.   1/2/3/4/5

Mental Toughness. Accepts strong criticism without feeling hurt; does not become easily upset when losing or playing badly; bounces back quickly from adversity; can take rough coaching; does not need excessive encouragement from the coach; does not necessarily depend on the team for a sense of belonging.   1/2/3/4/5

Coachability. Respects coaches and the coaching process; receptive to coaches' advice; considers coaching an important part of becoming a good athlete; accepts the leadership of a team captain; feels free to talk to the coach about ideas; cooperates with authorities.   1/2/3/4/5

Conscience Development. Likes to do things as correctly as possible; tends to be exacting in character; dominated by sense of duty; does not try to "con" his coach or fellow skiers; will not attempt to bend rules and regulations to suit his own needs.   1/2/3/4/5

Trust. Accepts people at face value; believes what his coach and teammates say, and does not look for ulterior motives behind their words or actions; free of jealous tendencies; tends to get along well with teammates.   1/2/3/4/5

Photo courtesy of Copper Mountain, Colorado.

"Anyone who thinks a kid can't get hurt skiing isn't a pediatrician, patrolman, or parent."
DR. DON OVEREND,
pediatrician, patrolman, and parent

17

HOW CAN YOU PREVENT SKI INJURIES TO CHILDREN?

Face up to it, children get hurt skiing. Scads of different reports from different physicians, statisticians, and the like come up with scads of different conclusions. One even suggests a skier has more of a chance of being injured if he takes lessons! Generally, as unconvincing as I've found these studies to be, the consensus seems to be that kids are every bit as apt to get hurt skiing as adults are. So if you've heard anywhere that kids are immune, forget it. If you believe they're less apt to get hurt seriously, forget it. It may be true that children, because their bones are softer, can walk away from accidents that would cripple an adult, but I suspect that this safety factor is offset by their greater tendency to put themselves into dangerous situations, or by the observable fact that they fall more.

I'd hate to put a probability factor on injury, because the reports don't even agree on how often adults get hurt skiing, or even on what you mean by getting hurt: a slight sprain? a cut from the edge of a ski while falling (ranging from very minor to extremely serious)? a dislocation (far quicker to mend in a child)? For some reason, current folklore has evolved that the injury rate among skiers is "six per thousand ski days" (a recent study dropped that to four), but since this raises more questions than it answers I'm not sure it's relevant, meaningful, or viable.

I'm sure Dr. James Garrick, a noted Arizona orthopedist who's spent years trying to make order out of this chaos, would take sharp issue with my cavalier disregard of these findings, but frankly, I don't care. I know people get hurt skiing and that kids get hurt skiing—but until our systems of reporting and analysis get better we're essentially going to be able to say little more than I just did. Tom Montemagni, among others, deplores the lack of reliable data and has been pushing for some form of physical testing to learn what the danger areas are. Now we don't know. Period!

One important thing we do know about children's injuries is that if they affect the epiphyses—the growth centers at the ends of their bones—they can be very serious. This can produce uneven growth between healthy and damaged bones. This point was made all too graphically by both Dr. Overend at the Copper conference in 1978 and by Dr. Milton Wolf later that year at a conference of children's instructors at Mount Snow. I gather from what they said that these injuries aren't too common, but that these are the ones you have to worry about. A clean oblique fracture of the tibia will heal more quickly in youngsters than in adults, but a break in the growth center demands immediate and top-flight professional attention—plus a few prayers.

Another thing we know is that children below the age of twelve shouldn't wear helmets. At first blush this seems strange, since one would think helmets would help prevent head injuries. In fact, helmets exacerbate the fact that children carry a higher proportion of their body weight in their heads than adults do. Further, Dr. Overend has emphasized, few (if any) helmets on the market are designed with little children in mind, and the trailing edge of that helmet is as apt to snap their necks as to protect their heads.

The following are the few steps you can take to reduce the risk of serious injury:

* *Use ski brakes.* One of the great dangers in skiing comes from the pinwheeling ski, that two-edged sword swinging free and fast when a skier blows out of his binding but keeps the ski attached to his body by that ultimate Orwellian misnomer, "the

safety strap." (The "safety" it provides is to other skiers, much as a soldier's falling on a live grenade protects his buddies.) The ski brake substitutes discomfort (as in walking back up the hill to get the ski) for disaster (as in getting your head separated by a sharp ski edge).

* *Set bindings a tad loosely.* If it's true that many falls won't generate enough torque to release a binding no matter how perfectly the unit is designed, maintained, and set, as the researchers designing bindings tell us (see Chapter 10), then perhaps we shouldn't even consider this option. However, I tend to suspect that part of that disclaimer has a tinge of the self-serving about it; besides, no one denies that many injuries that occur at very low speeds (or even standing still) result from too high a setting. This is when a lighter setting will help, even though you increase the probability of prerelease at high speeds. The choice narrows to a triple-communated-spiral-fracture-with-a-reverse-layout-twist, if the bindings are set too tight, against a bad bruise from a prerelease (assuming you use brakes and avoid the pinwheel). In case you're curious, I set my bindings half-a-notch low, and I tend to ski fast. . . . Also, keep those bindings in good condition. All those injunctions for adults—keep road salt off bindings, lubricate them regularly (check with your ski shop), and recheck the settings every five days you ski (at the shop or with the ski patrol)—apply equally to children.

* *Buy boots that are neither too high nor too low in front.* I discussed this in the section on equipment, but it bears some repetition here. When and if the physicians finally conclude that children do (or do not) have a weakness one-third of the way up the tibia—and your

opinion is as good as theirs right now—the basic, decisive fact is this: If a fall develops enough torque to break something (other than the binding), you want that something to be the tibia, somewhere between the one- and two-third marks and preferably a nice, clean, oblique crack. (To your obvious retort, all I can riposte with is, I have kids too— and yes, I've heard the old gag: "What are you selling this year, leprosy?") But a cheap, low boot will put all the stress on the growth center and delicate joint at the ankle, and an expensive but too-high boot will transfer the stress to the growth center and fragile joint at the knee. A boot one-third of the way up will put the stress on the tibia. You choose among the three; it's your child.

* *Put rubber tips on the metal ski-pole endings.* That's self-explanatory, no? At least, grind the points down, or get one of the newer-design poles that don't look like spears. And make sure your kids wear goggles whether the tips are blunted or not. Personally, I agree with Barbara Roylance, director of the Winter Park children's program, who feels that youngsters shouldn't have poles below the "D" class level and the older children (ten or over) below "C" class. We can give you five good reasons why not, including coordination problems, but after she lists all those reasons, she admits we're fighting a losing battle and says, "At least try to teach them how to hold and carry poles safely, with the points down, so that they don't stab themselves, other skiers, or you in the parking lot or on a liftline."

I have no opinion on ski length as a function of safety. I've heard the "experts" discuss it both pro and con with no resolution. A longer ski will produce more torque than a short ski when caught in snow, but this puts more stress on both the leg and the binding. Which will go first? Tune in tomorrow.

Truly, I hate to sound so cavalier, but I really do accept as fact that children can get injured skiing and that equipment still has a long way to go where safety is involved. Jim Spring, one of the best equipment-marketing people in the ski industry, feels we're nearing a whole new generation of binding designs that will render obsolete even the best state-of-the-art units we now have. I hope he's right, because I have reservations even about the Tyrolia, Salomon, and Burt. Thus, we can't avoid injuries; all we can do is minimize the severity and pray.

This applies equally to problems like frostbite, because you're occasionally going to expose your child to severe cold. Proper selection of clothing and attention to layering and tucking will eliminate much of the risk, but you still have to watch them carefully, because children in action lose mittens and allow hat, goggles, and dickey to separate. Remember, even in weather as skiable as a minus-10° windchill, a child is vulnerable even though most adults aren't. On another level, you have to make sure a little girl's hair stays tucked in when she's riding a lift or else it can get caught on a T-bar or chairlift. In other words, the keys to safety in skiing are vigilance, attention to equipment condition and clothing, and luck.

Assuming injuries do occur, experienced skiers know that they should await the ski patrolman and get carted down in a sled. However, that doesn't mean that even the most knowledgeable skiers actually do this, and I wish I had a dollar for every one of us who's skied down the trail with a bad bang and a suspected who-knows-what.

So let's lay this out as a firm rule: If your child has taken a bad spill and seems to be in pain, wait for the ski patrol.

True, young kids often have a low tolerance for pain. A few years ago, we were all skiing at Temple Mountain in southern New Hampshire when Greg took a wicked spill and started screaming, "My leg, my leg." I immediately immobilized him, and two patrolmen appeared almost as quickly; we checked and found nothing wrong and Greg was upright in seconds, pain vanished miraculously, and off he went. A bit sheepish, I started to apologize to the patrolmen, only to be told I'd done exactly the right thing.

For those of you inexperienced in the ski world, the ski patrol are those skiers, usually in orange parkas with yellow crosses on the back and small emblems on the chest, whose job it is to check conditions on the trails (out west, sigh, they usually get to cut the first tracks in new powder), blow off potential avalanches, and provide temporary first aid to injured skiers. At most areas they constantly roam the trails in search of reckless or injured skiers, but at the larger areas special phones and/or patrol stations are maintained; they're usually marked on the trailmaps, which you and your child should carry.

Assuming you're not alone on a trail with an injured skier—child or adult—you can ask any passing skier (most of whom will stop and ask if they can help) to send up a patrolman and sled; then you wait with the victim. On those rare instances when no passing skiers exist—I can't remember ever experiencing that, but people tell me it does happen—you should carefully remove the victim's skis (*only if* it doesn't aggravate the injury), plant them uphill of the victim in a crossed upright position in the snow, make sure the victim is as comfortable *and warm* as possible (even using your own parka if it's not too cold), then ski down to the nearest callbox or hut. Then get back to the victim as quickly as possible.

But unless you're certified in first aid, don't try to help the victim, and don't move him. Most American ski areas are expert at handling the wounded, and none charges for the service.

Some authorities suggest that if your child is skiing alone, i.e., not with either parent, you should sign a release for emergency treatment and put it inside your child's parka. I'm a bit skeptical about that, lawyer that I am; the first-aid staff in the emergency room will do what they have to do without such a release while they try to find you. I'd just as soon make the on-the-spot decision about major treatment myself.

One last point on injuries: As mentioned earlier, one study a few years back concluded that taking lessons doesn't minimize the chance of injury (although superior ability does). The physician involved was as aware as you and I of the incompatibility within that logical imperative and had the grace to admit it; he also added a few other qualifiers that removed some of the sting. However, the "fact" of the basic comment has been repeated without the qualifiers and has been used to justify a refusal to take lessons "because they won't reduce the chance of injury."

Nonsense. If a consensus can be drawn among the putative statistical studies I've seen—one big IF—it's that strong skiers get hurt less than weak skiers until they reach the high-expert/competition level, where the injury ratio begins to ascend again. High-intermediate and advanced-recreational skiers appear to have the lowest rates of injury, and you and your children won't get to that level very easily without taking lessons. (Some groups of high-expert skiers, such as mature instructors and patrolers, are reasonably accident-free as well.)

The breakpoint in that sequence is where the lessons start focusing on the hotdog end of freestyle ("flips") or on racing, when in fact you shift from "lessons" to "coaching." Then you're entering the world of competition with its constant demands for "ten-tenths," which puts the skier into the category of halfbacks and hockey pucks. But don't equate that with taking lessons to become a better recreational skier.

In preventing injuries, ability helps and lessons help develop ability. It's that simple.

Part IV

The Teaching Method

INTRODUCTION

At some point, every book like this has to get into the "technical instruction" stuff about how we take a toddler-on-skis ("A" class) from those first tentative steps through the grades up to junior racer or freestyler ("F" class). If you listen to the experts from the instructors' establishment you've got to wonder, isn't the A-to-F progression too difficult for a mere youngster to master? Conversely, as you read some of the technical writing, you could also ask, is learning to ski really that dull? The answer to both questions is no, it's neither that difficult nor that dull. Left to their own devices youngsters can learn to ski reasonably well rather quickly and have fun doing it. But good instructors can teach them better and quicker and offer almost as much fun in the process. On balance, good instruction is the better option by far.

Youngsters, once they've acquired the barest rudiments of sliding, have a natural tendency to point their skis directly down the fall-line, pausing in their torpedolike progress only long enough to jump over obstacles like moguls, tree stumps, rocks, and fallen skiers, unless they decide it's more fun to ski around these obstacles, as close to them as possible, by converting them into a natural slalom course. Every so often, if they happen to sense that maybe they're going a bit too fast, young skiers may consent to make a barely perceptible check—a *turn* —until they're back down to cruise-missile speed, or until they fall. Youngsters right up through their teens measure the success of their ski days by comparing the number of runs to the number of falls, and if they could remember their "facts" in regular school as well as their skiing statistics, none of us would have to worry about their grades in arithmetic.

Skiing in the fall-line is how kids of all ages have fun. For the young ones, a fall is like getting a word wrong in a spelling test: not really important, except that Mommy and Daddy and the teacher won't like it, which in itself wouldn't be terribly important except that it might lead to not getting a candy bar or being "grounded" for an hour. So, when skiing with Mom or Dad, kids learn to moderate their fun just enough to keep the parent happy; they make the minimum number of turns acceptable to the particular parent in charge of that run, and dream of the day they can go off by themselves.

Children don't like to go to ski school after they develop a fairly low level of skills development—roughly, after learning the wedge. Many instructors call a child's concept of good *bad,* deride fun as dangerous or irresponsible, and describe good skiing as being able to make more and better turns. Undoubtedly, the child will find that boring and wonder when will this lesson end so he can go back out *skiing?* Woe betide the instructor who stops his class on the snow, gathers them around him, and says, "Now we'll learn how and when to plant the pole." The more imaginative kids have a tacit answer for him.

Lest you think this is the experience of one skiing parent with two aberrant children, let me tell you about a rather typical day I had a couple of years ago at Mount Snow with George Schissler. George has been around the track—skiing, ski-writing, and ski-parenting in Connecticut—a lot longer than I have. His elder son Dave is a quasi-former racer (they never *quite* quit) who's become a ski-writer himself up in New Hampshire, yet having survived this trauma intact, George fathered another young skier almost two decades later. One day, the three of us stood atop the slope watching George's and my youngsters bombing through dangerous late-spring slush with a total lack of concern. "A couple of scooters," Dave laughed, drawing scowls from George and myself. "Make a couple of turns,"

George yelled downhill, the paternal liturgy of hope; neither child reacted with any noticeable enthusiasm (or, for that matter, displacement). "Slow down," I yelled, the other half of the prayer, and the three of us laughed. Hopeless.

"How do you get your kids to go to ski school?" George asked me suddenly.

"Oh," I said, "I tell them that I'm writing a book and handling all the coverage of kids' skiing for *SKI,* and that I need their help."

"Does that work?" George asked, a glimmer of hope flickering.

"Yup," I said, "especially when it's coupled with the statement that if they don't go to school they're not going skiing."

"That's blackmail," George said. "I love it."

Meanwhile, the pair of them, in a typical ad hoc race, continued their "fire one, fire two" course down the hill.

The story had a funny reprise the following season. While I was out West, Dee took Greg and Alix up to Butternut Basin to ski and ran into George again. Greg immediately hooked up with George and his young son and spent the day bombing the black-diamond runs, while Dee and Alix headed for the easier trails. "How did it go?" I asked when I got back.

"I don't know," said Dee. "I didn't have the guts to watch."

"It went *great,* " Greg said. "We were skiing *faaaaast.* "

And that is what it's all about when you are nine years old. (Come to think of it, recalling a day I had at Keystone just about that same time, that's what it's all about for putative grown-ups also.)

Now, as I developed this pattern of extortion and coercion I learned several things about what makes a ski-school class tolerable to children—and that is the proper word: tolerable. On a scale of one to ten most children would rate an exceptionally interesting class as high as maybe three. Most rate zero. In the course of the next few chapters I'm going to recite the chapter-and-verse of the skills-and-technique progression of teaching kids how to ski—at least, the version SKIwee and the better ski-school directors are evolving. But some rules are universal: A good instructor keeps his verbal instructions to a minimum; tells the kids exactly what to watch (and copy) him do; does not make them aware of being involved in what educators call a "learning situation"; and gives them challenge and excitement. He also understands that the type of terrain conditions that chill even strong adult skiers couldn't bother a kid less.

If kids have another general trait, it's a desire to ski with a minimum of effort. Martin Marnett, who runs the adult Sugarbush Workshop for Centered Skiing, uses a great metaphor: "A sculptor of great talent was once asked how he fashioned such beautiful horses from a block of wood. 'I don't carve horses, I simply remove all the wood that isn't horse,' he said."

Parents are still carving horses, and the biggest problem children's instructors (and directors) have is with parents. "I have this recurring scene," says Tom Montemagni of Mount Snow. "I tell the parent 'Johnny just came down the Jaws of Death [an expert trail] with beautiful edge control.' 'Yes,' says the father, 'but when will he ski parallel?' "

I tend to be guilty of that, albeit less and less. Greg is essentially a lazy and efficient skier, a "scooter," and you better believe he finds the easiest effective solution to the specific terrain challenge. One day we were coming down off Big Spruce at Stowe on a wide, gentle catwalk and of course showoff Dad was short-swinging beautifully. I turned to check Greg who, right on my tails, as usual, was in a wedge. "Shame on you," I yelled. "On something this easy you're using a snowplow. Why?" Then I stopped, realizing that he'd been running straight in a slightly wide-track parallel, checking with a small wedge when he started going a bit too fast, then dropping back into a wide-track run. Nothing wrong with that; he was totally in control, using his edges only as much as needed.

Another time, earlier that season, Tom, Greg, and I were skiing on Standard, a gentle slope, when, not to mince words, Mount Snow was Mount Ice. Even Tom was having his problems and I was totally out of control. Greg was in tears on the top half; nothing worked. Yet even before Tom did, Greg shifted to using a flat ski and banking his turns off the inside of the moguls rather than trying to carve on the outside as I was doing. As Martin Marnett might say, I left a lot of wood on the horse that run, while Greg had pared it down to the mane.

The new instruction theories accept this concept and adapt teaching to how children really ski. They also realize that not only four- but seven-year-olds may not be ready to learn the wedge, or that they may not be into learning anything *that day* because it's too cold or too gray or they didn't like what they had for breakfast. Furthermore, the good instructors know that the program musn't penalize a child, even subtly, for choosing to remain inside rather than to ski.

Not a bad idea if parents adopt the same attitude.

18

WHAT ARE THE BASICS OF CHILDREN'S INSTRUCTION?

About a year ago, on a hot and muggy September day in Manhattan, I was walking through midtown with another writer after testing the new AMC Eagle for our respective magazines. Since he and his wife are pretty fair country skiers, we started talking about skiing—specifically, some of the new methods of instruction.

"I just don't like them," he said.

"They're a hell of a lot more efficient," I said.

"I just prefer to watch one of those old-timers moving gracefully down a trail, moving like a bird," he said. "It's so pretty."

I agreed that perhaps some of the smooth, bobbing, rhythmic grace had yielded to aggressive efficiency of late, but I held firm that the new insistence on making a carved turn produced a technically superior and more versatile skier. "Maybe," he said, "but they all look like racers, not skiers."

He's right. How can you argue with one man's sense of esthetics? But the new-method instructors are also right. I feel the new theory is far superior to the old final-form concept, but maybe we'd better stop calling it the American Teaching Method (ATM) and, instead, face up to what it really is and label it the Modified Racing Technique. ATM is not a logical, sequential development from the old Austrian-based system that began with Hannes Schneider in New Hampshire in the late 1930s and peaked with Stein Eriksen everywhere in the late 1960s; this is now a discontinued if historically important dynasty, known as the Modified American Technique (MAT).

Calling the new ATM "Racing Technique" would suggest more accurately that modern recreational skiing technique (ATM) began with Jean-Claude Killy in the 1968 Olympics and has peaked, so far, with the racing style of Ingemar Stenmark as adapted for the advanced-skier workshops. Its hallmarks: efficiency; control; the carved turn; balance, edging, and pressure. The old emphasis on unweighting—an upward or downward movement of the body to initiate a turn—is passé; if it remains at all, like an appendix, it's little more than a rebound as you shift from inside edge to inside edge while changing direction. (Unless, of course, you find yourself in heavy snow, when jumping can still be the most efficient way to turn.)

Although switching from the old to the new has created problems for adult skiers (a point many of us have noted in a series of articles these past few years in *SKI* magazine and elsewhere), we all feel experienced skiers should make the effort to learn it because it is superior; it allows you to ski faster, cleaner, simpler, with far more control and far less effort than the Modified American Technique ever did with its heel-thrusting, hip-swinging, jack-in-the-box bobbing. It also gives you more weapons in your arsenal to counter changes in conditions and terrain. I'll agree we may have sacrificed some grace and poetry along the way, but efficiency is beautiful in its own right. One fact is true: Today's advanced-intermediate skier is stronger than most experts of a decade ago, and it's not just because of the superior equipment (although the hardware has helped to foster the new technique).

Children have had no problems adapting to this new theory. It more accurately mirrors what they do by instinct anyway: Faced with a sudden need to change directions, a child with some time on the snow will stand on the inside edge of that turning ski without thinking about it, often lifting the nonturning ski off the snow, keeping the two skis a reasonable distance apart, and using his legs independently. He'll do the least amount of work necessary to ski under what he feels is "control."

Under the Austrian-based system, instructors tried to drill youngsters (and adults) away from their instinctive reactions into a preconceived series of "final forms": snowplow, stem, christy, parallel, short-swing, like that. The ultimate aim was to do everything with the two skis glued together, and a skidding/sliding tight-parallel was deemed superior to an aggressive, carved stem, even to a strong, widetrack parallel, because a tight-parallel was the more advanced "form" or "technique." Inefficiency was all right so long as you looked pretty. The amazing thing is that some ski schools persist in this silliness, and many good recreational skiers have trouble spreading their skis apart because they feel it doesn't look "pretty."

Kids don't care how they look as long as they feel good, the girls as much as the boys. They don't even think about looking pretty unless they're forced to, and they stop thinking about it as soon as the pressure is removed. In the course of producing this book, I asked Rick Godin, an excellent photographer, to shoot Copper Mountain's sequence of instruction. He chose an exceptionally strong young skier and ran him through the paces, and in the photos that ten-year-old neo-racer looks as if he'd never graduated from a wedge—unless you know what to look for. You can see that his turning ski *is* on edge and the hips and knees *are* inside the turn, but the other ski sits wherever the boy felt most comfortable putting it. If we were to examine sequence photos of Stenmark or Phil Mahre to see if their skis are glued together, or even parallel—forget it. Today, form follows function, as it should, and kids are nothing if not functional.

For the past several years, both the good adult advanced-skier workshops and most of the children's learn-to-ski programs have keyed on this modified racing technique. The only group hesitating to make the switch are the adult learn-to-ski programs, which are still wedded to the inefficient but highly marketable foot-swiveling Graduated Length Method (GLM) and its offshoots, mainly because the areas bought all those little skis and still have to use them. As these skis begin to break down through use, GLM is slowly phasing out. Thank Ullr. Thus, don't be surprised if your child is being taught differently than you were (or are) under MAT or GLM; if anything, he's being taught better (method and technique) under ATM.

The idea behind ATM is not to produce racers. It's to produce skiers who move with the efficiency and control of racers, and who learn how to *feel* when the ski is doing its job. Since kids intuitively rely more on feelings and sensations than adults do, much of the early concentration in today's children's programs is devoted to developing confidence in their reliance on what and how they feel. It's the antithesis of GLM. This racing-based program holds youngsters back a bit longer initially, but allows them to move forward more quickly when they're ready —at which time they often leap from "B" to "E" class so quickly you can't believe it. In contrast, GLM pushes adults quickly from "A" to "C," where you can remain forever. GLM doesn't do anything for children who never took to it anyway.

Now, whether a child (or even most adults) can make a *pure* carved or racing turn is another question. Some of us, including Werner Zwahlen, ski-school director at Waterville Valley, believe a child isn't strong enough to counterflex a ski until he's roughly twelve and therefore isn't "carving." Tom Montemagni feels that even if that's true, a child will make a more efficient turn by keeping the ski on its edge rather than by skidding— and then, when he *is* strong enough, he already knows how and doesn't have bad habits to break. I tend to agree.

THE STATUS OF KIDS' INSTRUCTION

Children have always gotten the short end of the stick in American ski instruction—not so much at individual areas (many of which have long had good programs) but rather at the formal, national level of the Professional Ski Instructors of America (PSIA), which certifies instructors and writes the manuals that detail what should be taught and how to teach it. However, PSIA has never written a manual specifically aimed

However, PSIA has never written a manual specifically aimed at or for children, seeming to presume that they are simply little adults and what's good for Dad or Mom is good for their son or daughter. This is nonsense, as any parent well knows, but these days we're beginning to suspect the converse may be true: What's good for the son or daughter may be good for Dad or Mom. But that hasn't been the PSIA way.

This is not meant to demean PSIA. With all the changes in technique and teaching/learning theory that have be-sieged PSIA in the past decade, the multi-thousand-member association covering instructors at more than 700 ski areas from coast to coast has had trouble producing and updating a universally interchangeable program for the admittedly more important adult-skier market. Any organization that size, that rooted in tradition, is going to be slow to react to change, especially since changes were minor for thirty years, until the early 1970s. But the week in which Killy destroyed Karl Schranz in the 1968 Olympics with an exciting, flashy, successful new style, he also destroyed the validity of the Austrian-based MAT. Sadly, no one was listening when Killy commented that the inspiration for his new style was watching how children ski.

Since then, it's been Killy bar the door. Racing technique exploded, to the point where Killy himself noted recently that he couldn't possibly beat Stenmark or Mahre, peak against peak, with his technique against theirs. This shift—from the Austrian up-unweighting turn to the Killy down-unweighting turn to today's stepping-skating-rebounding turn—is nothing short of a revolution. It's been aided by the new "weapons," the radically improved skis, boots, and bindings (even poles), and has put PSIA on the spot to adapt these rapid-fire changes in technique to the recreational-skier level.

At the same time, theories about how to teach have been battered by an even more radical revolution. American skiers were never overjoyed with the Austrian-autocratic "Ziss iss how ve do it" approach, also known as "Bend zee knees, Two dollars pleez." The success of Tim Gallwey's *Inner Game of Tennis* begat emulation in all participant sports, and his *Inner Skiing*—the book and the program—took off like a flash. A parallel movement evolved based on the Oriental martial arts, Zen, Transcendental Meditation, and the like—the whole "head game"—and is best exemplified by the Sugarbush Workshop for Centered Skiing. Inner/Centered had, as its core, a "do it and feel it, don't think about it" credo that sharply contrasted with the Kantian analysis mandated under the Austrian system. Suddenly, PSIA's ruling clique faced as major a challenge to its recommended teaching method as it did to its approved skiing technique.

With its whole adult program under attack, you can imagine where this left children in PSIA's hierarchy of priorities. Fortunately, several good children's instructors and program directors were pressing PSIA to do for children what it was trying to do for adults. Tom Montemagni wrote a manual for the eastern region of PSIA and Pam Stenmark for the Rocky Mountain region, neither of which was adopted, although they fueled the movement.

On a local level, all manner of good programs for kids were evolving across the country—I could name twenty and not touch them all—but they lacked that core of interchangeability. What Copper Mountain was doing didn't mirror what Mount Snow was doing, and a young skier in "E" class at Snow might have to revert to "C" class at Copper and might get run off the hill at Stratton. This was the old pre-PSIA situation adults faced in the 1950s now revisited upon the young skiers in the 1970s, and it was a mess. Pity poor Greg and Alix, as they bounced from one program to the next while I researched this book and the articles for *SKI* and elsewhere. Their only consistent teaching/skiing program was their father, who's hardly qualified for the American Demonstration Team.

Ultimately, several of us throughout the writing and instruction fraternities felt the time had come to solve this problem—and thus, SKIwee evolved.

WHAT IS SKIwee?

Forces converge, trends coincide, people group accidentally in the right place at the right time, and, presto, you make a movement. *SKI* magazine, like *Skiing,* has long had a deep involvement in covering new methods and techniques of skiing: *SKI* pushed for codification of the chaotic system of the 1960s into the Modified American Technique, moved quickly behind the Killy/Georges Joubert "French Way," gave significant encouragement and coverage to the Inner/Centered workshops, backed GLM (perhaps overmuch), sponsored "Women's Way" seminars, and more. Thus, getting deeply involved in a program to teach children was nothing unusual, and I think *SKI* beat *Skiing* to the punch by about fifteen minutes.

Further, *SKI* (again like *Skiing*) had the clout to put together at short notice a conference of the top people in their specialties and has a track record of creating and marketing successful satellite recreational-skier programs such as NASTAR. Finally, some of us at *SKI* just happened to have young children going through the system at that time, producing the vague feeling that all was not going as well in this ski-school sector as it should be. Hence, in March 1978 at Copper Mountain, we convened the first national conference on children's skiing, at which time SKIwee was conceived. In September 1979, a 100-page illustrated syllabus emerged, four areas were signed up (NASTAR started with less), a sponsor (Hot Gear) enlisted, and all systems were go. By the fall of 1980, SKIwee was in about fifteen areas.

SKIwee is an all-encompassing syllabus/program/workbook/system that the areas' instructors are supposed to follow after attending a clinic run by the SKIwee staff. It addresses everything from equipment and clothing to terrain gardens, imagery, games, and language to skills and technique. It specifically defines which drills and skills will be taught in which classes, and how; it spells out the procedure for putting children into the proper class (the old "ski-off"); and it even tells instructors how to eat lunch with their students. Perhaps most significant of all, SKIwee includes a report card, much like the Red Cross swimming program, that checks off the skills or techniques the child has mastered so that another SKIwee area knows where to put that child when he shows up.

It took Bob Kunkel, Tom Montemagni, and Christi Northrop more than a year to complete the job, and the result, first crack out of the box, is a solid "5" on that ubiquitous 1–10 scale—not too far behind the current level of adult skiing after two decades of tinkering, and a solid notch ahead of the Sugarbush workshop during its first year in 1976.

The key point is that SKIwee has identified and tried to supply the need for a universal system of children's instruction to be taught at the nation's areas. As weaknesses appear—and I'm sure they will—they'll be solved . . . until, of course, a whole new theory of something—technique, skills, teaching method, or equipment—arises to challenge SKIwee's very existence and essence. At this point, though, it's the best game in town.

19

WHY AN EMPHASIS ON SKILLS?

The cleft between "technique" and "skills" has been fostered by advocates of the new children's systems and mentioned earlier in this book; it has been hyped to create an impression, make a point, and boost the marketing thrust. In fact, the innovative ski instructors have taken two words whose formal definitions aren't that disparate to emphasize a difference in how to teach, not in how to ski. To clarify: Copper, Mount Snow, Waterville Valley, and SKIwee offer a "skills approach" to teach the American Teaching Method.

After all, the goal is still to slide down a snow-covered mountain on two skinny pieces of plastic with a maximum of élan and control. A ski can do only so many things, good or bad, en route to the bottom. Good skiers have always relied on the edge, used the ability of a ski to rebound from reverse camber, developed a sense of balance and flow, and accepted the idea that you edge into the hill (and angulate away) if you don't want to fall off. The skiing techniques have changed to reflect the improvements in equipment: We don't have to corkscrew into exaggerated comma postures today because a stiff-sided plastic boot, a nonrocking binding, and a live ski with tortional rigidity lets us ski quite well from the hips on down.

Methods of instruction have begun to catch up. "Skills" are in because "skills" work. You could say that "technique" is fading, or that "technique" has been subsumed under "skills," or that "skills" are a better method to teach "technique." It doesn't really matter how you phrase it. A difference exists between a "skills approach" and a "technique (or final form) approach," but it has nothing to do with how a ski descends under control, or in how a skier makes it descend under control. The difference is one of teaching approach.

As we mentioned, the key to skills is efficiency, underscored by simplicity, subtlety, and sensitivity. You still have to log a fair amount of mileage before you can ski well. You still have to keep hips and knees inside the turn and bend the other way (angulate) at the waist, and a little counter-rotation doesn't hurt (although these days we call it "anticipation" and "initiation"). You still plant the pole *before* you start the turn or, if you prefer, *to* start the turn; it's another semantic difference, and a good instructor is still going to jump all over you if you're planting your pole late (although these days he does it with subtle imagery and a pleasant smile). To make that point more firmly: An excellent instructor at Pat's Peak told Greg to plant his pole at the *end* of the turn! Same thing, same idea, different way to say it.

What the skills approach does is to break the skiing action into basic components of (a) edging or edge control, (b) pressure control, and (c) steering. Properly done, these three skills are taught as the basis for all levels of skiing, classes "A" through "F," and to explain all maneuvers, from basic wedge to advanced short-swing, racing, and freestyle. The strength of the skills approach is that it develops an "awareness"—I'm beginning to hate that word—of how a ski feels when you make it do the job it was designed to do. You don't analyze it to death (as most adults tend to); you feel it and you do it. Instructors deeply into the Inner/Centered game ask, in effect, do you think about how you walk? No, you just do it. How do you turn a ski efficiently? You make it carve. How do you make a ski carve? You just do it. How do you know when you're doing it right? When it doesn't skid. How much angulation? Not too much or too little. How much is that? Well, how do you walk?

All skills-approach drills are designed to create this feeling of knowing when you're doing it right. The closer a skier is to the age when he learned how to walk, the easier this feeling is to instill. A two-year-old can learn how to feel how to ski as naturally as he learned how to feel how to walk. It will be harder for a six-year-old beginner, harder still for a teenager, and almost impossible for an adult novice. Yet at the other end of the scale, an advanced recreational skier of any age who has logged high mileage and developed a sense of confidence in his ability to make skis work can be lured into trying to reach the little-child ski-as-you-walk state of near-intuitive reaction, especially when he's told that achieving this state of grace will push him into true expert status. (We all need some of that.)

Another problem that prevents an adult beginner from accepting this childlike state is something called expectation levels. The adult (and older teenager) wants to get on that lift as soon as possible and begin to ape his fellow adults high on the hill, and if he's delayed by doing easy drills at ground zero for too long he begins to feel cheated; the lessons, as they say, become "counterproductive." Youngsters don't have that hangup; they like to play, and if they're having fun at ground zero, they're not going to be in any hurry to get up the mountain. (Alas, their parents won't be quite so accommodating at $10 the lesson.) A good children's instructor can develop the basic skills in a solid day (two days for the less athletic kids) of games and drills on the flat and in the terrain garden, while an adult instructor hasn't the flexibility and freedom to do that. It's a very fundamental point, and if you see your child still playing games at the base on Tuesday, don't despair. By Friday he'll be flying.

What are these skills: edging, pressure, and steering?

EDGING

When I started skiing in the late 1960s, I asked the instructor, after that first exhausting hour-plus, what's the essence of skiing? What makes it happen? "The edges," he said. In the hundreds upon hundreds of days I've spent skiing since, I've never forgotten it. I also haven't mastered it, except on rare days and runs and turns.

We all know what the edge looks like: It's that inset sliver of tempered steel, preferably sharp and clean, that borders the black or clear P-Tex bottom. The edges, in the words of the SKIwee preamble and syllabus, are like the "claws of a cat"— a lovely image, especially for children—and when they are extended they grip, or hang onto, the snow and the side of the mountain. (It also, according to Alix, means that they're "sharp and strong.")

However, when they're retracted, the edges let you slide smoothly down the mountain on top of the snow (assuming your ski bottoms are tuned). Thus, if you like a Zen-type approach, an edge is present even when it's absent: They're extended when you traverse, turn, or climb, and retracted when you run straight.

But you don't extend the edges as if they were an on-off light switch; rather, you adjust them as if they were a rheostat. What controls that rheostat is the amount of angulation at knees, hips, and waist, and, as you get better, ankles and shoulders and even the head. That rheostat is a subtle switch, and all skills-approach drills key on developing this rheostat.

Beginning instruction starts with simply walking around, first off skis, then on them; then it moves quickly to shuffling along ("Make believe you're a train"). The initial sequences first develop the flat-ski sensation (retracted-edge) by having the children make short, straight runs down onto a flat or slightly uphill runout; this stops the skier without his needing any skills. The next sequences key on developing the extended-edge sensation as the children climb (herringbone and/or sidestep), then use a wedge, first to stop, then to turn. At this point, the drills begin to overlap with those to develop pressure control.

PRESSURE CONTROL

A very bright writer named Denise McCluggage commented that the great problem in illustrating a book or article about skiing (or tai chi, tennis, or any movement sport) is that a picture stops the movement at an artificial position, interrupts the flow and creates the false illusion of a "proper position." Movement, flow, balance, and change are everything; static positions are nothing. Drills that focus on pressure control develop this sense of flow and change.

A ski, as we've mentioned, is a sensitive machine with many different properties; further, different skis work differently. What distinguishes the true expert from the rest of us is his ability to get on an alien ski and, with a few adjustments in pressure, know how that ski will perform under a wide range of conditions. Children can also adjust quickly, although they can't explain why and how.

The reason is sophistication or instinct in pressure control. This breaks into two subskills: position and weight.

* *Position.* Virtually every ski is marked with a midpoint under the ball of the foot that dictates where the bindings are mounted, and now that boots have that same notch (or should), the guesswork has vanished. A difference of even half an inch or a centimeter fore-aft in boot position on a 200cm ski can change how that ski turns. However, that presumes that the center of your balance is over that notch and that you're applying pressure downward directly over that center point. If you are, you have the full length of that ski pressed into the snow. Too far forward you lose the tails. Too far back you lose the tips. This fore-aft pressure is another rheostat, because as you're skiing you may want to unweight the tips or tails at different points in a turn or to adapt for different conditions and angles of decline.

     Pressure is also applied from side to side to extend the claws. The combination of fore-aft and side-to-side is part of pressure control, and the same movements apply equally to the most rudimentary wedge turn and the most advanced racing turn. The more you press forward and incline to one side, the sharper that turning ski bites and the more aggressively you turn. This reaches its peak when you lift the nonturning ski and focus all your centrifugal force on the inside edge of the turning ski, but it's equally at play when you apply maybe 5 percent more angulation to the turning ski in a beginner's wedge.

Pressure control, especially combined with body position and initiation—how you start the turn—is where today's top instructors focus much of their thinking and imagery. "Pressure control is enhanced by standing against the ski rather than on it," Tom Montemagni says, echoing a statement instructor-writer and U.S. Demonstration Team member Stu Campbell had made earlier in *SKI*. "This is what happened to you [meaning me] when that instructor [Martin Marnett of Sugarbush] told you to 'throw your hips down the hill.' You're getting your body away from your skis," (extreme angulation and early initiation) "which will cause a higher [degree of] edge sooner in the turn. This is a real trust move, and kids without lots and lots of mileage don't go for it very readily. But once they feel the results they never go back to just standing on their skis." Sure, it's a rather esoteric concept, but to get that young "E" or "F" class skier to execute and to feel that maneuver comfortably means he should have been playing with its basic sensation as early as "A" class.

* *Weight* (known at an earlier time as "unweighting"). Proper pressure control these days also involves learning "independent leg action," which means that you're using both legs all the time and doing different things with each. This is not a simple concept, especially if you were schooled in the Austrian technique. Look at

it this way: Assuming you have the proper length/ camber of skis, they are perfectly flat on the snow when your weight is distributed equally between the two. The moment you apply more weight-pressure on the turning ski, you counterflex it (see illustration on page 117) and allow the other ski to flex upward. This means the two skis are turning at different rates in different arcs, which strongly suggests you get a little distance between them or else the tips may cross. (This becomes most apparent in powder.) By shifting and standing on the previously nonturning ski and stepping off the turning ski, you change direction (assuming you also lean the other way). You've released the weight-pressure on one ski and applied it to the other. You get a little natural "unweighting" as you step from ski to ski as the previously counterflexed ski rebounds into its normal flex-camber position, just as a bow does.

The skills approach spends a lot of time in the early lessons teaching the proper positions and sensations so that the child can develop both aspects of pressure control. A major problem children have—adults also, but not to the same degree—is a tendency to sit back on their heels in a knock-kneed posture, putting the skis on edge but not applying pressure to the tips that, like front brakes in a car, do most of the stopping. There's nothing wrong with a knock-kneed position in a wedge (although you might infer there is from the SKIwee syllabus), provided the child is also applying forward pressure. Initial drills are keyed to the child's learning to apply that forward pressure, both in using the stopping/turning wedge and in climbing.

Can you turn without using pressure control? Sure. You can jump around a turn, which is essentially what you did in the up-unweighting MAT theory; you can kick your heels around the turn in a skid, the essence of GLM, or you can simply muscle your way through by swinging your shoulders and arms and hips and like that, which is how most intermediates turn and which is what Sugarbush finally broke me of to a large degree. Almost all skiers use a combination of the four methods —jump, heel-thrust, muscling, and pressure control—depending on the instant challenge, but the fine skiers rely mostly on pressure control with a small residue of jumping and/or heel-thrusting and only rarely a touch of muscle (except in crud or heavy powder). The higher the reliance on pressure control, the better the skier.

STEERING OR CHANGING DIRECTION

Dave Sanctuary, who wrote the kids' manual for Copper (see Appendix), prefers the word "steering"; SKIwee uses "changing direction." Neither is supposed to be synonymous with "turning," which involves using all three skills at the same time.

The best image I've heard to describe "steering"—and everyone uses it with kids—is: "Pretend your knees are the headlights on a car. They have to point in the direction the car is turning." SKIwee recommends drawing happyfaces on the kids' knees to illustrate the idea graphically, but that may be excessive for older kids. Basically, the skill you're trying to develop is pushing and leaning the knee forward and into the direction you're turning—or, as Martin Marnett describes it, letting the knee lead the turn.

One problem area in "steering" I don't feel the "skills" people have solved—so far as imagery and description are concerned—involves the feet. To a person, the instructors oppose a heel-thrust and favor a foot-swivel in making a turn. It sounds good and a thrust is a no-no—except that as I watched my own feet doing both maneuvers with skis on, I saw no discernible difference in what actually happens. (You can see a difference in soft snow using just your boots.) Further, if your skis are close together and you want to fall into a wedge, you better thrust your heels apart because if you just swivel off the balls of your feet, you're going to cross your tips; somehow, I do not believe this is a pattern anyone wishes to foster unless he enjoys watching people mash their noses in the snow. This is an area that remains to be defined and refined.

What they're really saying is that good skiers "ski off the balls of their feet," the point where you would swivel. This is more of a mental set than a true physical difference: It gets the skier thinking about standing upright on the balls of his feet rather than sinking back on his heels. Just thinking about your heels in skiing is self-defeating, and a good instructor at Pat's Peak told me that when you're sinking backwards, "Push onto your big toe." Same idea.

That pretty well covers the basics of the skills approach. Each has a series of subskills involving initiation and sequence and balance and leverage, different theories of pressure to adapt to different types of terrain and snow conditions and the like, and these will develop as we trace the sequence. Now, let's talk about some other aspects of the "new approach."

20

WHAT ABOUT FEAR?

"Kids have no fear. That's why they learn to ski so well and quickly." I've heard that myth so often that, if I didn't have any children of my own, I might almost believe it. The weaknesses in that statement are so obvious I almost hate to mention them; but in the interest of journalism:

* "Kids" aren't some monolithic, interchangeable group of parts. "Kids" is kids, and any parent who has even two children, produced by the same combination of genetic structures, is quite aware that children are very different from each other. Since both of mine were weaned at ski areas, neither exhibits any fear of sliding on snow; but each approaches skiing differently and I can tell you now, with some degree of certainty, which one will be content to become an expert recreational skier and which one will want to race. We have friends who ski almost as often as we do and one of their children loves skiing and the other hates it. We have another friend who loves to ski but his elder child absolutely panics when the skis begin to slide; no way that child has even begun to overcome fear. Some kids have less fear than others, even as me and thee. What is true is that young children are less apt to be frightened by the prospect of falling than adults, but even that isn't an absolute.

* A little fear is a good thing. It gets the adrenaline pumping, which is very useful on a tough run, and it

defines parameters of safety: You don't go on trails that are too far above your ability level. Sometimes I wish some children had a little more apprehension, especially as they approach blind ridges and huge moguls. It's here that an adult influence—parent and instructor—is necessary to instill a low level of this apprehension, also known as the "rules of the road" or, more graphically, "You do that again and I'll remove your lift ticket."

*   That no-fear myth is usually followed by canard no. 2: "Kids don't have as far to fall," or "Their bones are so soft they can't get hurt." On the second, obviously invalid comment I'll refer you to the pediatricians and orthopedists, but you better believe kids can break and sprain things. If you're a parent, you know that when they fall and hurt themselves they *hurt,* and I'm not about to quantify pain. . . . As for that "farther to fall" business, that presumes that Wilt Chamberlain will hurt himself more when he falls than you or I will, and while I can't speak for you I don't believe that nonsense. (Besides, as they say about jumping off tall buildings, everything past the first five floors is ego.)

So let's get rid of these canards forever, and accept the fact that a good instructor has a dual role vis-à-vis fear: (1) to eliminate the panic or terror some children feel when they begin to slide; and (2) to instill a bit of defensive apprehension about trees, lift-towers, other skiers, and trails that are too far above the skier's ability level. This isn't an easy job, and it's complicated by the fact that some children progress faster than others, physically and psychologically.

MILEAGE

One factor that is as true for children as it is for adults is that the best way to learn how to ski is to ski. Put in hours and miles. Develop confidence in a conditioned reflex, based on experience, that can override the slower analytic process. (Even allowing for differences in natural ability, the best winter drivers are those who've logged 10,000 miles a season under dire conditions for a decade or so.) This experience factor is necessary for tangling successfully with any alien element, and snow—in its many divers forms, from deep light powder to solid-glare ice—is indeed an alien element even without those long, alien things on your feet.

The good instruction programs accept the need for mileage and build some free skiing time into their skiweek programs (it's obviously impossible on a one-shot weekend lesson). Free skiing means exactly that: The class lines up at the top of a slope or trail that the youngsters have skied before and takes off. The instructor's role is more shepherd than teacher, although the good ones manage to impart a few effective, casual "tips" along the route. Many programs and instructors also take the kids down trails that they haven't skied before on a follow-the-leader basis, which is a silent lesson in learning how to read terrain as well as a drill for logging miles. Some instructors like to play games on the way down, anything from "tag" to "let's see who can make the most turns" or "nicest jump over the bump." (Don't shudder; if there is a universal about children, it's a fondness for leaping over tall buildings in a single bound, and a good instructor uses this efficiently and safely.)

A group of youngsters skiing together covers a lot of ground, because most kids like to ski with other kids. Children in a mob egg each other on, and they know who's the best skier and either follow him or challenge him. A good instructor or director tries to limit the disparity between best and worst in a class, either by creating two separate groups or by juggling the class lineup every morning. This friendly competition is a healthy experience, and even left to their own devices two strange kids the same size and age will immediately race down the hill to see who's better, then do it again and again and again, especially if they're reasonably close. Sure, you've got some loners, and if you leave them alone they'll probably become the best skiers in the lot because skiing is essentially a lonesome sport; but generally, children are gregarious.

Since many children also like to ski with their parents, you can help generate mileage by letting your children ski. Unless you're a fine skier with a solid technical background, don't be too quick to offer helpful tips; ask the instructor what he's been working on and how you can help develop that skill, drill, or movement, but recognize that you're doing your children just as much good if you let them have fun and "go for it." I know it's tough to do, and your unique relationship with your children and your skiing ability will dictate how you handle the venture. But don't spoil it for them by too much screaming; remember that it's almost as important that they *do* it as that they do it right. Mileage is its own reward.

GAMES

One unfortunate tradition that has persisted for five decades is the name "ski school." It's been a problem for adults as well, which is why many ski areas now call their programs for experienced adults "workshops" or "institutes" or "seminars." Adults don't want to go back to school, and, as parents know too well, kids don't greet it with a superabundance of enthusiasm either. Ask Greg if he wants to go to ski school and his eyes glaze. But he sure didn't mind joining the Mount Snow "Demonstration Team." Copper calls its groups "Junior Ranch," "Senior Ranch," and, for their regular weekend programs for kids from Denver, the "Copper Choppers." Winter Park has launched the "Graduated Kid Method," which is on the right track but not quite there. I'm still not in love with the name "SKIwee" but it beats "school."

Still, changing a name isn't going to solve the problem if the kids walk into the same old drill: "Copper Choppers" will produce just as many glazed eyes if the instructors start talking about "lateral displacement" and "initiation." The SKIwee syllabus has as many "don'ts" as "do's," and many of the no-no's focus on using technical language. What finally launched Alix on her first solo run was an hour-long lesson at the excellent Waterville Valley nursery in which she learned how to stop by playing "red-light/green-light"; had she been told, instead, that she was going to be taught how to stop by "dropping into a wedge and swiveling your feet," she would have turned off. She knew she had learned how to stop, you understand, but she hadn't known she was being taught. It's a signal difference.

This isn't a startling breakthrough, of course. Good instructors have been playing games with kids for more than a decade, even before Rudi Wyrsch popularized it in the early 1970s at Mount Snow. But until recently there haven't been that many good children's instructors. I remember one lesson Greg took at Mount Ascutney, Vermont, when he was about seven, in which (I learned later) the instructor told him to keep his shoulders square with the bottom of the hill and keep his hands forward—valid advice, to be sure, and totally appropriate for Greg's technique at the time, but he would have understood it equally well had it been delivered in Serbo-Croatian. What we had, as the warden said in *Cool Hand Luke,* was a failure to communicate.

Tom Montemagni, in one of his earliest efforts to create a children's manual for Eastern PSIA, wrote the following:

> Children are not small adults. The best method to teach kids is steeped in imagery and founded in movement. Use appropriate similes accompanied by explicit demonstrations, even descriptive sounds. For example, to teach hop turns:
> Simile: "Pretend you're a gorilla in darkest Africa."
> Demonstration: Climb up the hill and do hop turns coming toward the class and away from the class.
> Sounds: Ape-like grunts.

He also commented about a child's "insatiable urge to play ... that flows spontaneously and instinctively from every child. Play is a child's work. When they're playing, they're happy, relaxed, and constantly on the move ... but beneath the surface they're working, learning about themselves and their environment, and how to handle both. But this method of learning is non-conscious."

Once you accept that, play becomes the method of teaching, by using games and images. You talk to them in terms they understand:

* "Piece o' pizza pie." My daughter Alix, at age four and a half, did not want to learn how to snowplow ("wedge," if you insist). I tried my lexicon—"An A without the cross" (which had worked with Greg). "Upside-down V." "A slice of pie" (problem, Alix doesn't like pie). All she wanted to do was run straight. So, I dumped her on Nancy Alfaro at the Mount Snow nursery and told her Alix wouldn't snowplow. By the end of the session, Alix was tickled to show me her very good wedge, because the instructor had her doing a "piece o' pizza pie." Alix loves pizza and knows exactly what a piece of pizza looks like.

* "Ski on your tippy-toes." As with all children (even the strong skiers), Alix loves to ski sitting back. Tell her to get her weight forward, right? It's a waste of breath; her backside remained one-eighth of an inch above the tails. What did the Mount Snow instructor tell her? "To go faster [not true, by the way], stand on your tippy-toes with your hands on your knees." Instant success.

* "Hands like a helicopter pilot's." This one is courtesy of Greg himself. I noticed one day that whenever he hit frozen-granular (also known as Vermont powder) the tip of his turning ski began to wander because he didn't have enough weight on the shovel. A good cure is to keep your hands forward. Unable to create a decent image, I reverted to the old standby, "Follow me for a few turns and watch my hands." No real change. In the liftline I went through the technical hands-forward/weight-forward bit, with the usual blue glaze in his eyes as a result. Desperate atop the

trail, I started swinging the poles in a simulated hands-forward rhythm. "Oh," he said finally, "that's like flying a helicopter." "It is?" I asked. "Oh, sure," he said, "I see it on TV all the time." Success.

I can go through a long list of these terms—"Squash a bug" (swivel your ski), "make like a big bird" (unweight)—but since none will work with all children, what's important is the concept: Deal with your children in pictures they react to, and don't get locked into anyone else's images. The good children's instructors learn how to talk to many different kids, and you usually have to deal with only one at a time. But don't tell him to keep his shoulders square to the bottom of the hill, because kids barely know where their shoulders are. If you must, tell them to keep the bellybutton pointed downhill, because they know what that is. (To repeat an interesting corollary we mentioned earlier: Barbara Roylance of Winter Park recommends that if your child has trouble explaining in words what he learned in ski school that day, "have him draw pictures of it. Kids are amazingly accurate doing that.")

There is, however, one technical term they can relate to: "Let them run straight for a while."

APPENDIX

A TEACHING/LEARNING SYLLABUS

Sometimes I think we labor overlong on stressing the semantics, and forget the basics. They tell this wonderful tale about the early, creative days of Inner Skiing. A guy we'll call Harry was in one of those first classes, and after group therapy the night before and a heavy head session over breakfast, he felt *ready:* not for nothing the probing insights of coping like a coconut and soaring like a bumblebee. On the slope, even before the guru finished the first mantra, Harry took off, graceful as a stork, and before anyone could even say "Ommm," he was thrashing around in the trees, saved from serious injury only by a rapid reaction of wrapping his arms around the trunks.

"What happened?" the guru said when he reached the dazed Harry.

"Like, you know, wow, I felt it. My left shin was red and my right shin was green, and my knees were nutcrackers and wow, I was digging the turn, I could smell it and taste it from my bellybutton on down to the edge, it was going to be the greatest turn of all times."

"So, my son?" the guru said.

"No one ever taught me *how* to make the turn."

So, let's talk about the "how." On the following pages, courtesy of Dave Sanctuary's syllabus for the Copper programs, we have a short progression beginning with the first days on skis ("A" classes) up through the advanced-recreational stage ("E" class). The expert level is rather irrelevant because by that time the youngsters are eyeing the racing courses more than somewhat, trying freestyle, and making their own individual adjustments.

I'm using Copper's syllabus rather than SKIwee's because the former is about one-tenth the length and because the latter has far more technical detail than anyone except an instructor needs. The underlying theories and progressions are the same. So, without further comment, the following is the world of children's skiing according to Dave Sanctuary.

SKILL APPROACH TO TEACHING

DAVE SANCTUARY
Technical Director
Copper Mountain Children's Ski School

This paper is to be used as an aid in your everyday teaching at Copper Mountain. It is not exhaustive in its content, and it's not complete in its scope. It is merely meant to give you some ideas on how to introduce and work with the basic skills in our teaching system.

The idea behind this theory is that the three skills discussed are absolutely basic to all of skiing. Without them we cannot accomplish any level of success. They are critically important not only to the advanced expert, but also to the first-day beginner.

The "skill" approach to teaching skiing is quite new; so new in fact that there is little, if anything, printed and available to us. It has been thoroughly analyzed and practiced by the PSIA Demonstration Team, and has become highly touted as a most effective concept of teaching. In the near future, much additional information will become available through the efforts of PSIA and its technical and methods committees.

In order for us to get the most from the attached outline, it is imperative that we all have a few simple understandings of what that is, what it is not, and how we're to use it. Therefore, please note the following:

1. All new material should be introduced by a static demonstration whenever possible.

2. This is not an isolated system of instruction, but is meant to be used in conjunction with the other parts of our system, such as (a) introducing the entire maneuver first, (b) use of psychology, (c) importance of kinesthetics, (d) use of inner game theory, (e) classic ATM, etc.

3. Whereas many instructors will think of these suggestions as exercises, they are not, at least in the basic concept of teaching "skills." They are suggestions for introducing maneuvers and/or ideas in an effort to fulfill the student's need to learn THAT SPECIFIC SKILL, which he must do if he is to progress.

4. There are many more ideas for teaching these skills than are included here. With your help and ideas, we'll be expanding this outline significantly.

5. There are many skills which are not mentioned in this outline. These are referred to as "sub-skills" and are quite important in their own right. However, they are not considered to be basic.

DESCRIPTIONS OF CLASS LEVELS

CLASS "A"
   – first time on skis through introduction of wedge turn
   – should never be repeated by a student
   – at completion of class, all students should be able to cause a change in direction in a wedge position
   – should be comfortably familiar with basic terminology, equipment and its care, what happens next

CLASS "B"
   – probably second time on skis
   – primarily concerned with wedge turns at various radii and various speeds

– class devoted to mileage, becoming more familiar with relationship between feet and skis, confidence

– should terminate with introduction to skidding through spontaneous christy, terrain sideslipping, stem turn, etc.

CLASS "C"

– entire time spent dealing with basic christy

– begins by working on either spontaneous approach to christy or a definite matching approach to christy

– should take student through being able to make a basic christy from the fall-line

CLASS "D"

– almost entire time spent dealing with refinement of basic christy—some tangents to be pursued

– begins by working on basic christy from the fall-line

– is completed when student can adequately perform an advanced basic christy (matching before fall-line, preferably from traverse)

– generally includes pole plant introduction

CLASS "E"

– centered around application of independent and simultaneous leg action

– teaches stem-step, downstem, parallel turns, parallel step turns, carving

– is the highest level most students will attain

SKILL APPROACH TO TEACHING EDGING, PRESSURE CONTROL, STEERING

CLASS "A"—Without Skis

Edging

1. Walk across slope on sides of boots—feel for edge of boots biting into snow—identify foot sensations.

2. Sidestep up the hill.

3. Standing on flat area, rock from one edge to flat boot to other edge and back—identify and memorize sensations and how they change.

4. Spray snow by kicking snow with edge of boot sole.

5. Relate how knee movements cause edge, and how application of pressure to boot edge tends to cause knee to move in that direction.

6. Hop into and out of wedge position.

7. Have student vary the amount of edge pressure while standing in a wedge position.

8. Practice skating-type movements pushing off from one boot edge and landing on other boot—then edge that boot and push off to the other boot, and so on—make certain student understands that each boot must be edged before he can push off.

Pressure Control

1. Feel back of boot and tongue of boot by applying forward and backward lower-leg movement. Relate to sensations present in foot, shin, leg.

2. Stand on one foot with eyes closed—relate to how it is easier with knees flexed and body relaxed.

3. Introduce ready position on skis by associating it with ready position of other sports.

4. With eyes closed, have student apply varying degrees of pressure on the front part of his boot (toes?) and the back part of his boot (heels?).

Steering

1. Have students pretend to twist one foot, then both feet, as though they were trying to extinguish a cigarette on the snow, assuming cigarette is under the middle of the foot—relate to sensations in the toes and at heel.

2. Standing in a wedge position, have students apply pressure against one side of their boots with their toes—then their heels—then relate to how sensation should be noticed at both parts of their feet.

3. When introducing steering in this manner, do not seek strong pressure changes, as this will invariably cause a strong hip movement—sensations are relatively subtle, but definitely noticeable.

CLASS "A"—With Skis On

Edging
1. Repeat any maneuvers done without skis which are applicable.
2. Slight traverse across hill for brief distance.
3. Straight run stressing flatness of skis.
4. Straight run to gliding wedge and return.
5. Traversing gliding wedge.
6. Stepping out of gentle traverse or straight run.

Pressure Control
1. Repeat any maneuvers done without skis which are applicable.
2. Positioning body weight in proper location by having student push off with poles into straight run on level.
3. Review ready position, and relate how body movements change pressure point along ski.
4. Straight run changing pressure from front of ski to middle to rear to middle to front and so on—have students seek out what they feel is most comfortable.
5. To further instill the understanding of pressure recognition, do straight run while alternately releasing most pressure on one ski, applying it to the other, then reverse—stress that this pressure change should be centered around legs rather than leaning upper body from side to side.
6. Go from straight run to wedge position with definite extension motion—with definite flexion motion.
7. To further instill ability to recognize pressure changes, have students go from flat skis to edged skis while standing still and/or while traversing—stress pressure sensations, not edging.

Steering

1. Repeat any maneuvers done without skis which are applicable.

2. Pick up ski and twist it—relate to relative difficulty in feeling true twisting (steering) action in foot.

3. Place ski lightly on snow and repeat above movement—student will now be able to feel action of foot in boot.

4. Work on controlled positioning of ski while picked up off the snow—vary degrees of tip and/or tail crossing with eyes closed—make certain students know how to recognize the location of their ski with eyes closed.

5. Hop into wedge position and back—relate to equal amount of steering on both sides.

6. Straight run to wedge and back.

7. In wedge position, have students attempt to steer their toes toward an object on their left or right.

8. Pay particular attention to student being able to steer inside foot while changing directions.

9. Wedge wiggle.

CLASS "B"

Edging

1. Strengthen fundamentals learned in "A" class.

2. Alternate holding and release of edges in traverses and in gliding wedges.

3. Use terrain to overcome weak edging, therefore encouraging skidding.

4. Encourage wedge turns in narrow stance with enough speed to overcome weak edge—possible spontaneous christy.

5. Change edge on inside ski after completion of wedge turn.

6. Change edge on inside ski during last third of wedge turn.

7. Do wedge turns with extremely large arcs, then do wedge turns with small arcs.

8. Begin wedge turn, then tighten turn.

9. Rapid alternating of strong and weak edging throughout wedge turns.

Pressure Control

1. Encourage outside ski pressure by angular body positioning.

2. Practice matching skis by standing in a traversing wedge position with pressure on both feet—then match inside ski to outside ski—stress the added pressure noticed on outside ski and/or the reduced pressure noticed on inside ski.

3. Practice matching inside ski to outside ski while traversing (strong edging in traverse not desirable).

4. While doing linked wedge turns, have students alternate application of pressure on back, front, and middle of ski—intent is to have student learn to regain balance—should be done with quick movements.

Steering

1. Have students do very long radius wedge turns, then short radius wedge turns—relate to difference in application of steering inside their boots.

2. Wedge wiggles at varying speeds.

3. While doing a wedge turn, stop steering, then begin steering again, then stop it, then start it, etc.

4. Do wedge-turn garlands across the fall-line to encourage directional change as a result of steering.

5. Choose terrain that will allow a wedge turn to occur even with the weakest of steering by student.

6. Practice matching of inside ski while traverse sideslipping.

7. Practice matching of inside ski while traverse wedging.

8. At completion of wedge turn, have student steer just the inside ski to match.

CLASS "C"

Edging

1. Vertical sideslip.
2. Forward sideslip.
3. Long sideslips with various degree of edging.

4. Spontaneous introduction to slipping because of terrain change (road transitions?).

5. Increase edging quality along with steering as basic christy advances by static introduction and further practice.

6. Increase emphasis on stronger edge before and after matching.

7. Alternate sideslipping and traversing—make slow transition and rapid transition.

Pressure Control

1. Use of breathing rhythm—inhale and extend to enter a turn, exhale and flex to match and complete.

2. Use of terrain to add pressure reduction at time of matching.

3. Basic christy stressing change of pressure from one ski to another.

4. Use of forward pressure on boot tongue to facilitate continuation of turn and controlled skid.

5. Show students the relative ease in matching when speed is slightly increased.

Steering

1. Increase steering through wedge/match garlands.

2. Change sideslip to a controlled arcing turn.

3. Decrease original turn radius by increased steering.

4. Concentration on inside leg steering before, during, and after matching action.

5. Traversing wedge to hockey stop.

6. Sliding wedge to hockey stop.

7. Change relative position of tips and tails while sideslipping through steering of feet.

CLASS "D"

Edging

1. Hold downhill ski edge while stemming uphill ski.

2. Ramover wedge entry (therefore faster, therefore encourages a momentum-type turn).

3. Tighter turns through edge emphasis.

4. Uphill christies (fans) from fall-line done by going from flat ski to edged skis, then all steering (this introduces the concept of "edge, then turn").

Pressure Control

1. Introduce extensive unweighting while standing still and incorporate into basic christies; purpose is to facilitate edge change (resistance?).

2. Have students experience varying degrees of pressure changes by extension unweighting, by trying an extreme jump upward through a very subtle little upward action—practice eyes open and closed—practice static matching of skis with various amounts of unweighting (eyes open and closed).

3. Practice basic christies at various matching points with emphasis on the edge change/match coinciding with the pressure (unweighting) change.

4. Snow printing—static followed by moving—attempt to force (pressure) letter on front of ski into snow to leave mark on snow—stress kinesthetic awareness through boot and foot pressure.

5. Practice forward, backward, and neutral pressure on skis while doing sideslips (vertical and forward).

Steering

1. Encourage steering of inside ski (foot) sooner.

2. Sharper turns via increased edging/steering.

3. Linking of basic christies.

4. Uphill christies (fans) approach for carving.

5. Hockey stops.

6. Encourage turn entry with narrower wedge.

7. Have students try strongly steered turn uphill just before their regular basic christy—that is, wedge or stem the uphill ski, then make a short turn uphill IMMEDIATELY followed by their regular basic christy.

8. Basic christy followed by an immediate stop—have students attempt to stop as soon as their skis have been matched.

CLASS "E"

Edging

1. Wedging while alternating strong edging on inside of one ski and flattening of other, then reverse.

2. Promote increased edging quality through use of the uphill christy (fan) by having students edge, then turn—edge, then steer.

3. Static introduction of angulation (body positioning as related to edging).

4. Stem-step on very gentle terrain—almost down fall-line, with emphasis on stepping from edged ski to edged ski.

5. Static practice for downstem platform.

6. Downstem garlands for stable edge set/platform.

7. Use of proper terrain for "automatic" wide-track parallel turn.

8. Uphill christy (fan) to promote wide-track parallel turn.

9. Skating.

Pressure Control

1. Introduce flexion unweighting by relating to what student would do if he stepped on a hot coal or sharp stone in his bare feet—immediate flexion.

2. Rebounding from downstem by doing downstem turns from the fall-line—start "straight down" hill.

3. Use of moguls for aiding downstem/rebound action.

4. Rounded moguls for reducing resistance (pressure) during edge change for wide-track parallel turns.

5. Practice stem-step turns on flat terrain—stress kinesthetics —concentrate on pressure changes.

6. Extension unweighting practice for wide-track parallel edge change (practice static and dynamic, eyes open and closed, exaggerated and subtle).

7. Small turns down fall-line with extension unweighting— gentle terrain.

8. Snow printing—described earlier.

9. Traversing steep trails over "large" moguls for absorption-flexion-extension-ski/snow contact.

10. Introduce how steeper terrain and bumpy terrain can aid skier in edge change.

Steering

1. Review edging suggestions for "E" class— cannot totally disassociate edging and steering at this level.

2. Total carving from fall-line in parallel position.

3. Single-ski steering with good speed on easy terrain (that is, make as much of the turn as possible on just the outside ski).

4. Pivot entry on mogul for wide track.

5. Linked wide-track turns on flat terrain for emphasis on foot steering (relatively flat ski).

6. Extreme wide-track position (skis very far apart) doing long-radius parallel turns—causes extreme carving.

7. Linked downstem turns for strong steering.

GLOSSARY

ATM, or **American Teaching Method.** The current teaching/ skiing method advocated by PSIA, ATM puts a high premium on the carved turn and racing technique and has begun to recognize that skiing is an emotional, intellectual, and intuitive pastime as well as a physical one.

BINDINGS. These are the expensive and intricate machines that attach the skis to the boots. Recently, the better bindings have included **ski brakes,** which allow you to eject completely from the binding (and the ski) so that the ski can't hit you (or other skiers) when you fall. Most authorities feel brakes are an improvement over the older **leashes,** often miscalled **safety straps,** which kept six-feet-plus of tempered steel with a sharpened edge hooked to your ankle and spinning quickly in what was called a **pinwheel,** which was as apt to cause a serious injury as the fall itself. See Chapter 10.

CARVED TURN or **carving,** occasionally known as the **racer's turn** and more frequently as the **barroom turn,** as in "I made some great carved turns today." In theory, it means that every centimeter of your turning (inside) edge passes over the same imaginary spot in the snow and that the ski doesn't skid at any point in the turn; it is the ultimate turn so far as efficiency and control are concerned. It also rarely happens consistently even with the best skiers, but good skiers execute it to a higher degree and more frequently than weaker skiers.

CHECK. A maneuver to reduce speed, either immediately before or as the first part of initiating a turn. With children, alas, it often comprises the totality of a turn.

FALL-LINE. The most direct route down any slope or trail, the one that a rolling ball (or aggressive nine-year-old) will seek. The closer you stay to it (jumping bumps along the way), the faster you go and the less physical work you have to do to turn. It also does great things to the pit of the tummy.

GLM, or **Graduated Length Method.** A product of the late-1960s ski-teaching revolution, this method put adult beginners on very short skis, then slowly "graduated" them to longer skis until, ideally, everyone was on the proper length of ski he'd have been on had he begun in a more traditional school. It never quite worked that way, and most GLM students stopped at shorter lengths, especially since this movement corresponded with the short-but-happy life of the short-ski craze. Children never took to it, fortunately, since their skis are inherently shorter than adult models anyway. GLM technique is still rather controversial, especially among purists.

HERRINGBONE. A reverse-wedge position (tails together, tips apart) used to climb hills. It is more efficient (at least faster) than a sidestep, and it demands that your thighs be in pretty good condition.

HOCKEY STOP. A rapid change in the position of the skis from fall-line to traverse, accompanied by a quick shift of the weight to the edges closest to the uphill. This is that dramatic turn-stop that sprays snow all over other skiers and is among the earlier maneuvers young skiers try to master. It is very efficient under all conditions except deep or wet powder, where you can break every bone in your legs if you try it.

MAT, or **Modified American Technique.** This was the first officially codified method of skiing and teaching approved by PSIA, dating back to the late 1960s, and was essentially based on traditional Austrian methods with an emphasis on "final forms." It survived for a long time and still has followers at many American ski areas, but overall it has yielded to the current American Teaching Method (ATM). See Chapter 18.

MOGULS, or bumps. The most controversial, humbling, frustrating, and written-about situation in skiing and technique, moguls are sometimes caused by terrain configuration but more often by skiers. They are those (often huge) bumps of hard snow on a slope or trail that tend to insist that you turn right now or fall on your tush. A gang of them is called a **mogul field**—in polite circles—and the description is often accompanied by pejorative comments about "the GLM skiers with their @ #$% short skis" who made the distances between the bumps too narrow or too short for "us good skiers with long skis."

PARALLEL, or parallel turn. Although it technically refers to any maneuver where the tips and tails are the same distance apart in either a straight-running or turning mode, "parallel" traditionally refers to that position where the skis are no distance apart, i.e., "glued together." This is very pretty to watch on easy terrain, but it tends to be highly inefficient on difficult terrain and has been largely discredited the past several years.

PSIA, or Professional Ski Instructors of America. The certifying and manual-writing association that regulates thousands of ski instructors (and instruction) at the 700-plus ski areas in the United States. It's a powerful group, and as with any large association tends to be run by the conservative wing and constantly challenged by the younger radical wing. All in all, it responds far more quickly than most groups of this size and type.

SHORT-SWING, occasionally still called wedeln. A series of linked turns close to the fall-line, which often resembles a series of minute checks rather than a series of completed turns—especially when young, aggressive skiers do it.

SIDESTEP. A method primarily for climbing, but sometimes for descending, a slope or trail. Put your skis at 90° to the fall-line, then edge into the snow with the edge closest to the snow, in effect creating stair-steps. The variation most used for descending is called a **sideslip,** where you then release the edges from the snow and slide sideways on the skis' bases, slowing or stopping by edging back into the snow. It's slow but certainly effective unless you're on ice, where it's almost useless and potentially dangerous.

SKI DESIGN and nomenclature. A ski has three main parts: the front, usually known as the **tip** or the **shovel;** the mid-body, often known as the **waist;** and the rear, usually known as the **tail.** Viewed from the top or bottom, the tip and tail are wider than the waist, and the degree of narrowing toward the center is called the **sidecut.** Viewed from the side, the tip turns up at the very front and touches the snow at the widest point; the mid-body arches up in the center in what is called its **camber;** the tail touches the snow at its widest point before it, too, turns up at the end. Viewed from the bottom, the ski has a plastic (P-Tex) base surrounded by thin, sharp, highly tempered pieces of steel called **edges.**

SKIDDED TURN, occasionally known as **sliding.** The opposite of carving. Essentially, it means that the tail of the ski is coming around the turn faster than the tip because the skier is using the flat bottom of the ski rather than its edge. It is usually not an efficient or controlled turn, especially on granular, icy, or difficult trails, but it's fine for easy cruising and even the best of skiers do it on occasion (only they call it the "flat ski" technique). Initially, this was called a **christy** or **christie.**

SNOWPLOW or **wedge.** Also known as a "piece of pie," an "A without the cross," an "inverted V," or a "Christmas tree." Tips are together, tails are apart. In most progressions the wedge is the first position in which a skier learns to control his skis to make turns or stops. A wedge is an inefficient weapon compared with other positions or techniques.

STEM TURN. In many progressions (although declining in popularity), this is the next stage after the wedge and/or the wide-track parallel. Begin in a parallel traverse position (wide or tight), then displace either ski (different systems or progressions prefer one or the other) to form a wedge to make the turn, then bring the skis back into a parallel. Despite its falling into disrepute, it can be a very effective maneuver in tight, difficult situations. In fact, if you analyze racers' techniques, you'll see they use a highly efficient and controlled stem turn most of the time.

STEP TURN. What racers and expert skiers call a stem turn, with the signal difference that the good skier steps up onto the turning (inside) edge of his uphill ski and transfers all his weight to it as part of his step; it is often accompanied by a quick lifting of the other ski off the snow. A highly efficient maneuver, it demands confidence and commitment. Its effectiveness in bumps is hotly debated.

TRAIL RATINGS. Trails are no longer rated "novice," "intermediate," or "expert," as they had been originally. Because of insurance-liability problems, trails today are rated "easiest," "more difficult," or "most difficult" on each mountain, and the signs to depict the three grades are green circles, blue squares, and black diamonds respectively.

TRAVERSE. Moving across rather than down the trail or slope, usually with the skis in a parallel position, is called traversing. It delays rather than solves the problem, because at some point even in an open bowl you run out of slope and have to turn.

WIDE-TRACK PARALLEL, or railroad tracks. A more advanced position/control than a wedge, this has both skis pointing in the same direction ("parallel") but a good distance apart. Some progressions start with this and ignore the wedge completely, which deprives a child of that necessary weapon.

INDEX